Paper and Spit

To PAT

Paper and Spit

FAMILY FOUND: HOW DNA AND
GENEALOGY REVEALED MY
FIRST PARENTS' IDENTITY

Don Anderson

ISBN: 1544606982
ISBN 13: 9781544606989
Library of Congress Control Number: 2017903824
CreateSpace Independent Publishing Platform
North Charleston, South Carolina

Foreword

THERE ARE ABOUT FIVE MILLION people in the United States who have been
adopted. Many of those people do not know who either or both of their
birth parents are. Don Anderson's book provides a gripping account of
his journey as he discovered first his birth mother and then later determined the identity of his birth father. Don's story reads something like a
diary, taking us day by day through this process. The reader can feel as
if he is right with Don as the discoveries unfold. Don provides a detailed
insight into the emotions he felt as he was going through this journey.
One can follow each twist and turn of the path that Don goes down as
he uncovers one new clue after another. This approach makes the reader
feel as if he is reading a riveting mystery novel. However, in this case,
the story isn't fiction, but is rather a striking example of the revelations
that many adoptees experience as they try to determine who their birth
parents are.

Don received valuable assistance from excellent genealogists such as
Susan Baird, Emily Aulicino, and Lisa McCullough in this journey. Don
is fortunate that both his birth father's family and his birth mother's
family accepted him with open arms once he discovered who they were.
Unfortunately, this doesn't happen each time that an adoptee discovers
who their birth parents are. I have helped a number of adoptees find their
relatives using DNA analysis and I know from personal experience that
some birth parents want to have little or no contact with their children

who were given up for adoption. However, even in those situations, I think that the adoptee can have some sense of closure in terms of at least knowing who their birth parents are.

Don's story highlights the role that DNA testing, particularly autosomal DNA testing, has been playing in recent years in assisting adoptees in their quest to figure out their biological ancestry. Not only can adoptees determine who their birth parents are from DNA testing, but it can also offer valuable clues as to one's ethnic ancestry. In Don's case, DNA analysis confirmed that he has Irish and Scottish ancestry, but that he didn't have any Native American ancestry as was suggested by the initial summary that he received from the adoption agency.

Although I was not adopted, I feel a personal connection to Don's story since I live in Portland where Don lives, went to high school in Salem where Don's grandparents lived, had parents who attended Oregon State University in Corvallis where Don was conceived, and have a strong love for music. I also have quite a few patients in my medical practice who are adopted, some of whom have had very gratifying experiences like Don has had as they developed relationships with their birth parents once they discovered who they were.

If you are an adoptee thinking about finding your birth family, I would suggest that you pursue it wholeheartedly. Even if you are not adopted, I would suggest that you use this book as a springboard for diving into the topic of genetic genealogy, which I have found to be a rich and rewarding avocation over the past twelve years as I have used genetic testing to help trace my family tree. Genetics can be a key to unlocking your ancestry and you never know what you will discover is hidden in your DNA!

Sincerely,
Tim Janzen, MD

Acknowledgments

A LIFE-CHANGING JOURNEY IS RARELY a solo experience. The same can be said about telling a fascinating tale. I dedicate this book to my wonderful family for their support and unending patience as my ethnicity changed.

Diana
Denise
Doug
Danelle
David

My thanks and appreciation to Nancy's family for their immediate acceptance, continued support, and willingness to part with saliva in my search for Stuart.

Margaret
Tom
Malcolm
David
Sue
Bruce
Cathy
Carrie

To Stuart's family for believing in me from the get go, instant generosity, and introducing me to the man who is alive in me today.

Keith
Claire and Jim
Randy
Gary
Joann
Steve

And finally, my gratitude to a group of individuals that played pivotal roles at crucial moments...moments that made the difference between quitting and moving forward, stopping and continuing, giving up and going on with confidence.

My Friends and Mentors
Susan Baird
Lisa McCullough
Robert Liguori
Connie McKenzie
Emily Aulicino
Richard Hill
Brenda Braden

Special thanks to Danelle Dullum for back-cover photo of the author and to Steve Smith for the book cover design.

Belonging to a family, tribe, or clan is magnetic. We all are driven by desire to belong, feel loved, and gain acceptance. I pondered my heritage…

Where do I fit in?

Pedigree Chart

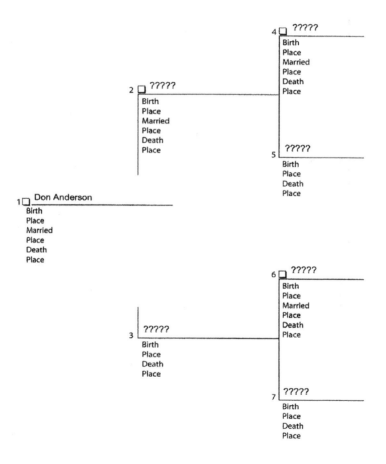

16 ☐ ?????
Birth

8 ☐ ?????
Birth
Place
Death
Place

17 ?????
Birth

18 ☐ ?????
Birth

9 ?????
Birth
Place
Death
Place

19 ?????
Birth

20 ☐ ?????
Birth

10 ☐ ?????
Birth
Place
Death
Place

21 ?????
Birth

22 ☐ ?????
Birth

11 ??????
Birth
Place
Death
Place

23 ?????
Birth

24 ☐ ?????
Birth

12 ☐ ?????
Birth
Place
Death
Place

25 ?????
Birth

26 ☐ ?????
Birth

13 ?????
Birth
Place
Death
Place

27 ?????
Birth

28 ☐ ?????
Birth

14 ☐ ?????
Birth
Place
Death
Place

29 ?????
Birth

30 ☐ ?????
Birth

15 ?????
Birth
Place
Death
Place

31 ?????
Birth

January 2, 2001

I DIRECTLY FACED THE DOOR. I rang the doorbell and heard footsteps from inside the house. What would happen? I held my breath. The door opened and from behind the screen, a tall, older woman appeared, dressed in a white blouse and blue slacks. Her kind, friendly face greeted me. She asked, "Can I help you?"

Taking a deep breath, I gathered my thoughts. I then started with the first of three phrases I had worked so hard to perfect.

"Is Margaret home?" She answered, "I'm Margaret."

"Do you have a sister named Nancy?" "Yes," she said.

"She is my birth mother." Wanting to show my earnestness, I simultaneously mentioned and pointed to the birth certificate in my hand. I continued by assuring her that this wasn't a scam. I was stopped in the middle of my sentence. This was it. I wondered what she would say. Margaret's words caught me by surprise. "I really felt that this day might come. Would you please come in?"

Almost six years earlier, I had made the decision that would forever alter the course of my future: the decision to begin searching for my birth mother. It was a decision forty-nine years in the making. One of the most important questions in my life was about to be answered. It all started with a response to a form I had mailed to the adoption agency that handled my placement. But this journey began many years earlier, with the birth of a baby.

ADOPTION

"I want you to know that you are adopted, and we can take you back anytime we want to." Those were the first words I can ever remember hearing.

They were spoken to me by my adopted mother when I was five years old. By the tone of her voice, I knew that she meant every word of it. They may be the only words I remembered from that age, leaving a monumental impression on my young mind. They were unforgettably repeated by this woman many times. Being returned to the orphanage often echoed in my thoughts, as would being rejected for the second time in my short existence. Unforgettable.

I was born in April 1951 and surrendered by my birth mother to the Albertina Kerr Adoption Agency in Portland, Oregon, two weeks later. Toward the end of October, I was adopted by a couple who lived in southwest Portland. For the first few years, I had virtually no memory of my early life.

Although the return trip never took place, those words sounded real to me, nonetheless. I couldn't count the number of nights I cried myself to sleep. The fear of being taken back *was* real. Was I wanted? Was I loved? The bonding that took place with my parents was based on fear, not love. Loving me for me and meeting my needs were not the reasons I was adopted. Because of this, my world would be colored by uncertainty for many years thereafter.

The issue of adoption needs to be addressed. Adoption may be thousands of years old, and countless books and articles have been written and stories told about it along with several discussions. People adopt children for many different reasons, ranging from wonderful—wanting to provide for a child's needs, to terrible—providing status or to having a child to work to support a family. Adoptees have expressed their perceptions as have birth parents, particularly birth mothers. Birth parents surrender children for various reasons—being too young or otherwise unable to care for a child, or simply because the child is unwanted.

"Sealed" records were typical at the time of my adoption, which centered around the birth certificate. Birth mothers were told their babies would have a much better life with their new adoptive families. And the standard phrase of the day was "They should put all of this behind them." Once their children were surrendered, they all could have a normal life.

I had yet to read about, or talk with a birth mother who was able to do that. Studies have shown that babies know their natural mothers, and are aware of separation after it happens. They are taken from the mother who gave them birth. And the real tragedy in all of this that these infants had neither the voice nor the ability to object.

I have great respect for those who have adopted for the right reasons—the primary one being to love and meet the needs of the child. If prospective parents had any other reason for wanting to adopt, they might want to reconsider their motives for doing so.

Regardless of how the adoption experience turned out, almost every adoptee I have spoken with, read about, or seen on TV reality shows and YouTube has had the same response when asked about wanting to know about their DNA heritage. The answer is "Yes." It's as simple as that...or is it?

There were three main reasons adoptees did not look for their birth parents: (1) fear of offending or alienating their adoptive family, (2) fear of being rejected by their birth parents, and (3) fear of their birth parents having passed away.

Birth parents also had four main reasons for not wanting to find the children they surrendered years before: (1) memories connected to the original surrender of their child being too painful to revisit, (2) fear that their child was angry with them for being abandoned, (3) reluctance to intrude or interrupt their child's new life, and (4) fear of violating the terms of legal adoption.

For adoptees, regardless of whether their adoption was a positive experience or not, one need was central and constant at some level—the need to know who their "first parents" were.

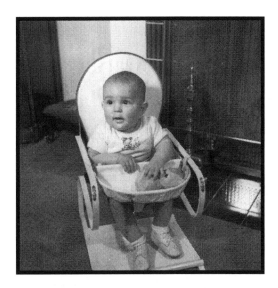 

SEARCHING FOR MY MOTHER

I wondered if my birth mother had ever tried to find me. This question had been in the back of my mind for a number of years, but finally took a prominent position in January 1995. At that time, my wife, Diana, was employed by Albertina Kerr, the same agency where I was placed forty-four years earlier.

Through the years, I received encouragement from my immediate family and friends to consider finding my birth mother. One friend, in particular, who would keep nudging me, was Susan Baird. She was a seasoned genealogist, and for many years had secretly wished that I would begin searching for my birth parents. On occasion, she would gently encourage me to begin the search. I had been resistant, but finally agreed to take the first step.

The agency provided a birth registry for adoptees and birth parents desiring contact. If both parties agreed, the agency would facilitate steps toward a reunion. One afternoon I called the agency. After explaining the reason for my call, the receptionist said that an inquiry form needed to be filled out, along with a payment of twenty-five dollars for processing my request. Then she cautioned, "I wouldn't expect too much. Usually, the information provided is sketchy at best. Good luck." It was not the greatest news to hear. I'm sure that was said to keep me from getting my hopes up.

One weekday, I traveled to Albertina Kerr during my lunch break and finished the paperwork by filling out the forms. On my way there, I wondered what information I might be given. And after I had it, then what?

After parking the car, I walked into the office and approached the receptionist. "I'm here to sign up for the birth registry." She handed me a form to complete. When done, I gave it back to the receptionist, along with the money. She said I would receive a letter with nonidentifying information in one to two weeks. I had taken my first step toward reunion. Had I done the right thing? Was I betraying my adoptive parents by beginning a search for my birth mother?

Two weeks later, a letter from Albertina Kerr arrived. I studied the envelope, wondering what the contents would reveal. After opening the top of the envelope, I slowly unfolded the page enclosed and read the following:

> *Your request for non-identifying information has been received, as well as your check for $25.00. As you were informed over the phone, the information is limited.*
>
> *Your birth mother was born in March, 1932 in Oregon. She is of Scottish, Irish, English, and German descent. She is reported to be a high school graduate. Her religious preference at that time was Baptist. Her health was noted as "good." However, she did have eczema on knees and elbows. She thought of becoming a nurse's aide, but did not wish to go to college. Her father was a college graduate, and her mother had two years of college.*
>
> *The only information about your birth father was that he had been married and divorced. He had some Indian blood, but it was unknown how much, nor was there any reference as to what tribe.*

**Since you have registered and there was no match, you can request a search through the State of Oregon. If you would like more information about a search, please feel free to call or write.
Sincerely, The Director of Community Services.**

Understanding each word on that page was of utmost importance to me. What was apparent? Most of the information was about my mother. In contrast, almost nothing was given about my father, which I later learned was quite typical. The receptionist at Kerr had cautioned me correctly. Her word "limited" described the contents accurately. Disappointment clouded over me. I let Diana read the letter and shared my feelings with her. I had hoped for more.

There was nothing more I could do for the time being. If my birth parents hadn't even made the effort to sign the registry, would they be interested in meeting me? Were they still living, or had they passed away? I wasn't ready emotionally to proceed into the unknown. A few days after receiving the letter, I decided to stop moving forward on something filled with so many emotional landmines. Too many questions, hardly any answers. I wasn't ready.

For the next three years, the desire to know the identity of my birth parents grew more and more. In January 1998, I was in a state of turmoil. My thinking was conflicted. The tape in my head kept playing over and over… what did I know for certain? Almost nothing. Not one shred of identifying information to go on further. How would I start searching for my birth parents? I didn't know who to talk to. My birth records were "sealed." They were inaccessible. The glaring question? What *were* the chances of finding my birth parents?

A FILE OPENS
In the early spring of 1998, a ray of hope appeared. Measure 58 was placed on the Oregon voter's ballot for the upcoming elections in November. If passed,

adoptees twenty-one and older in the state would have access to their preadoption birth certificates. Normally, ballot measures weren't of great interest to me, but this was the big exception. When an article related to the measure appeared in the paper, I eagerly read every word. This was really exciting to contemplate. Every adoptee in the state of Oregon would be given the option to unlock a secret—their birth parents' identities.

On election day, I proudly voted in favor of the measure. Apparently the majority of Oregon voters felt the same way. It passed by a wide margin. I was ecstatic! It wouldn't be long until this previously elusive document was in my possession. Wait...not so fast! Local radio stations and the *Oregonian* newspaper reported that four birth mothers had filed a lawsuit with the state to block what voters had approved. I was stunned. After a year of wrangling in the courts, the fate of the measure was still uncertain. So close and yet so far.

Frustration became my constant companion. Susan Baird must have had ESP. She called with a solution for me to consider. "Everything will eventually work out," she said in a reassuring way. "I just know that the court will make the right decision. Before you know it, you'll be holding your first birth certificate." Susan seemed so sure and was almost always right. I would need to borrow her optimism for the time being. She had some good news to support her feeling. She said that the state of Oregon would allow adoptees to fill out an application form, along with a payment of fifteen dollars to be put in a holding file. When the measure became law, those who filed early would receive their copies first. She suggested that I go to the office of Vital Records and do the same. I did, and then I waited.

Moving forward

On March 22, 2000, the Oregon Supreme Court declined to review Measure 58, effectively dismissing the lawsuit. Starting the second week of April, the first preadoption documents would be mailed out. I had to pinch myself to make sure this wasn't a dream.

A manila envelope arrived three weeks after the first day of issue. It was from the Office of Vital Records. This was what I'd been waiting for. The ball was in my court. Diana, our children, and friends all wanted to know the name of my birth mother. Once the word was out that the birth certificate had arrived, there was a clamor in the family to open the envelope. I looked at the envelope, with mixed emotions swirling in my head.

I told my family I needed a moment to think. Nobody really knew how I felt. Once I opened that envelope and viewed its contents, my world would change forever. Finally, it was time to face my future. I carefully sliced through the top of the envelope with a letter opener. Inserting my hand, I retrieved the paperwork. Once the birth certificate was in my hands, I began to read it.

Birth name—Richard Allan Blackstone
Date of birth—April 16, 1951
Time of birth—9:14 a.m.
The name of mother—Nancy Ann Blackstone
Age at time of delivery—19 years old
Place of residence—Corvallis, OR
The name of the Hospital—Emmanuel in Portland, OR

I was thrilled to finally have answers and memorized each piece of information. With the wait over, I began my search in earnest. In the scheme of things, acquiring my birth certificate was a small victory. The real work lay ahead. I had no way to predict the kaleidoscope of unexpected events that might await me.

I started with Nancy's place of residence, Corvallis. It was the home of Oregon State University. At one time, I considered going to school there. Those plans were dashed when my adoptive parents announced I would be attending Portland State University. I wanted to get away from home. They had other ideas.

I remembered Corvallis as a pass through, on the way to another destination. The town's status had changed. It became my destination for answers. Nancy's address was listed on my birth certificate. Was it a home, apartment, or college dorm? I called the Benton County Courthouse and asked where that information was stored. I was told it was located in the property records room.

Corvallis was ninety minutes south of Portland. On the way down, I had the feeling I was embarking on a new adventure. I was excited to see what I might discover. The courthouse was easy to find as it dominated the Corvallis skyline. Parking was conveniently located around the perimeter. I entered the building and received directions to the right location. The woman who worked in the records department led me to a vault-like room and pointed to the land records section.

I searched the shelf and found what I was looking for. After pulling the volume, I sat down at a table nearby, eager to see what I might find. Properties were organized by address, with newest owners listed first. I quickly found what I was looking for. The address belonged to a private residence. I counted a total of three owners. At the top was the current owner. At the bottom, the name recorded was Percy W. Blackstone. He must have been Nancy's father.

In 1925, he had purchased three adjoining lots, with the home on the center one. I had seen enough. I received directions to the address from one of the employees and eagerly set out to see if the house was still there. I was tempted to drive faster than the speed limit, but my cool head prevailed. As I drove by, to my relief, the original house was still standing. I quickly found a place to park, grabbed my camera, and took pictures. Mission accomplished, I happily headed for home.

My brain was on overload as I contemplated this new information. Nancy was eighteen at the time of conception, had been a resident of Corvallis, and just out of high school. That meant she most likely lived at home. I was optimistic: she might be easier to find than I originally thought. Were there any Blackstones still living in Corvallis?

My thoughts then turned to the birth father. Was he a student at Oregon State University? It was located in Corvallis. Or was he an employee of a local business? He had been married and divorced. Bottom line: what would it take to find him? I soon abandoned that line of thinking. For the time being, Nancy was the priority. Finding the father would have to wait.

The worth of a picture

Yearbooks were the focus of my next trip to Corvallis. I returned with Diana and made a stop at the high school. All archived copies were located in the school library. Judging by her age, Nancy would have graduated in 1950. My goal was to find her picture. Originally I wanted the medical history on the Blackstones. Now, I wanted to see what she looked like. How closely did I resemble her?

We found the school's main office, and after signing in, we were escorted to the library. The librarian greeted us and asked, "Can I help you?" "Yes. I had family members attending the high school between 1948 and 1952, and we were wondering about looking through yearbooks for their pictures." I refrained from mentioning I was looking for my birth mother, not knowing what the librarian's reaction would be.

Saying, "Let me show you where they are located," she guided us to the yearbook section. Diana started with 1948, and I began with 1951, just to be safe. We would finish with 1949 and 1950, respectively. Then one of us made the discovery. I was going through the senior class pictures of the 1950's edition, and bingo! I found her!

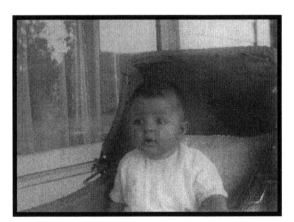 

This was the picture of a beautiful young woman. Studying Nancy's features, a visual revelation unfolded before my eyes. Her eyes, mouth, and head shape all resembled mine. Up until now, my children were the only ones that resembled me. That had changed. *I knew what my mother looked like.* The librarian allowed me to make copies of pictures that included Nancy. I now knew what my mother looked like.

During our trip back to Portland, I reviewed the original reason for finding my birth mother: I needed to know her medical history. No, that was not the truth. What was the truth? I wanted to find her and meet, if possible. I had believed finding my birth mother was virtually impossible. And I never met anyone that had done so. Why make the effort when a successful outcome was unlikely? And most importantly, why risk the heartache associated with a failure of this type?

Nancy's picture was a catalyst for change. I wanted to meet her. I needed to meet her. Could she be found? Was she still living? Was she willing to meet me? The answers would have to wait.

A SEARCH ANGEL APPEARS

I contacted Susan Baird and asked her what my next move should be. She suggested I begin attending Oregon Adoptive Rights Association (OARA) meetings, which were held monthly on the campus of OHSU (Oregon Health Sciences University) in Portland. Their mission was to help adoptees and birth parents navigate the challenges associated with search and reunion. Diana and I discussed whether or not to go, and then we decided to attend the next meeting, which would be held on December 20 at 7:00 p.m.

That night, we drove to the campus and headed for the main auditorium located in the library. Upon entering the auditorium, it struck me. I was not the only person interested in adoptive rights. There were around forty-five people in attendance. We found two empty seats near the back of the room. The concept of adoptive rights was new to me. I had no idea what to expect. What topics would be presented? My curiosity was killing me.

To start off, the organization's president extended a warm welcome and asked how many were attending for the first time. I counted ten hands including mine. After a brief business segment, it was announced that a birth mother would share "her story." This was a regular feature of each monthly meeting. A woman in her forties moved to the podium and began speaking.

She recounted her experience of giving birth and later surrendering her child, poignantly framed with regret and longing for reunion. Because of this birth mother's ordeal, I had a glimpse into the feelings of loss associated with her experience. It opened my heart to feelings of loss that can be just as overwhelming for the parent as the adoptee. This deeply touched my soul. I was speechless.

When her story concluded, a couple of people were introduced as professional searchers. Usually they charged for their services but offered to help those who belonged to OARA for free. Their specific purpose during the meeting was to help new members begin a search of their own. This sounded like a good deal, and we made a point of meeting one of them.

We were introduced to Donna, a birth mother herself. She then inquired about my circumstances and what I wanted to accomplish. I proceeded to share a short version of what had been done so far. I wanted to find my birth mother. But could she really help? Donna convinced me that she could provide the needed information to move forward.

THREE MILES AWAY

The next day, Donna was true to her word. She e-mailed my grandparents' birth and death dates. Percy W. Blackstone b. July 18 1897, d. January 5 1976, and Audrey M. Bagnall/Blackstone b. December 6 1902, d. July 2 1992. Holy smokes! How did she do that? And so quickly. Another key piece of information was included as well. Audrey's location at the time of death.

Where was the location? Clackamas County, just a few miles from where I lived. Amazing! This really got my curiosity going. Was Audrey living in Clackamas County at the time? Donna had also suggested what to do next. "You can view the obits (obituaries) at the Multnomah County Library on microfilm copies of the *Oregonian* newspaper." I thanked Donna for her help. Joining OARA had paid off. I knew where I would be the day after Christmas.

On December 26, I visited the library with the goal of finding the obituary. If Audrey died in Clackamas County, it would be in this newspaper. I asked for information on where the archived copies of the *Oregonian* were located. All archived materials were stored on the third floor. I began by looking at the film, starting with July 1, 1992. After loading the machine, I realized that her obituary would be in the edition a day of two after the date of death. I skipped ahead to the July 4 edition and spotted the obituary for Audrey Margaret Blackstone. I was glued to the screen. It included the surviving family members. Listed were her children: Margaret, Nancy, and Tom. Nancy had two other siblings! I mentally kicked myself. When Diana and I viewed the yearbooks at Corvallis High School, my goal was to find my mother's picture. I never thought of looking for siblings. A valuable lesson was learned that day!

The Blackstone family began to take shape. Progress had been made. Then, a sobering thought. What if Nancy had passed away? That was a real possibility. A speaker at an adoptive-rights meeting talked on this very subject. "Now is the time to start your search. If you wait too long, you may discover that one or both of your biological parents have already passed away." This was emphasized by her own experience. She delayed her search by six months. When she found her mother, it was two months too late. If only she'd started immediately, the outcome would have been quite different. I considered that while studying the obituary. I decided not to wait. Time was of the essence.

Finding the obituary became the easy part. Tracking down Nancy could prove to be much more formidable and time-consuming. According to the obituary, she had been living in Fontana, California. Would that still be the case? I attempted to verify the information. She had moved on and left no forwarding address.

Disappointed, I focused my attention on Tom, also a resident of California. While working with Tom's information, I realized that he wasn't the right sibling to locate. Margaret was. She had been living in the Portland area at the time of her mother's funeral. Chances were good that she still was.

Susan Baird gathered a list of names, locations, and phone numbers for all Blackstones who lived in the United States from the Internet. She called and made arrangements for me to pick it up. I appreciated her proactive creativity. Once the list was in my hands, I reduced it to Oregon residents. That proved to be a smart move. Going over the revised list, I was able to find Margaret's name and address in short order. I did a triple take after reading her address. I didn't believe what I was looking at. Her address was only three miles away from mine! How crazy was that?

The realization hit me—I had driven by her home hundreds of times over a number of years. In the future, driving down that street would have a whole new meaning. I grabbed the car keys and immediately headed for my vehicle—*I had to drive by.* As I approached her home, my foot went to the brake pedal. The living room window revealed a woman seated, watching TV. I realized that this was most likely Margaret. My search had taken a giant leap forward.

I arrived home, and told Diana about what I'd found. Then I called each of our children. They were really happy for me. Denise, our outgoing oldest daughter, volunteered to make the first visit. She even offered to take her firstborn, our grandson, along to make sure she would be allowed in! (It's hard to turn down a mother and her baby.) I thanked her for volunteering, but declined the offer. It was my responsibility to make the "first contact."

On December 28, I met with Susan and her husband Jim. I updated them on what had transpired and then discussed ways to contact Margaret. In the middle of brainstorming, Susan exclaimed, "Oh my gosh, I went to high school with a couple of Margaret's kids!"

I didn't see that coming. "Are you sure?" "Yes, I am. Let me get my year-books out, and I'll show you." She sounded positive. After an unsuccessful search, Susan decided to look later. She then rendered her opinion regarding contact. "You need to meet Margaret in person."

Chills went up and down my spine. I had anticipated writing a letter or possibly making a phone call at the very most. But meeting in person? My comfort zone had been breached. But the crazy part was I knew she was right. Susan sensed my heightened level of anxiety and reassured me it was the best way to facilitate a reunion. I left feeling better about her suggestion. With that settled, I was faced with choosing a date and time to act on this plan.

Did I know of anyone else that went to the same high school during the same time? I then remembered another friend, Randy Rowley, had gone there about the same time as Susan. It was quite possible that he also had known Margaret's kids. I phoned him and asked if he had his yearbooks handy. He knew right where they were stashed. I explained my need to see them. "Sure, I'd be happy to let you look at them. I'm home now. Do you want to come over?" My response was "I'll be right there!"

When I arrived at Randy's, his curiosity was killing him. I felt the same way. We both wanted to see their faces, but for very different reasons. For Randy, they represented former classmates and for me, family. First, he wanted a longer version of my story. I decided to humor him. He was amazed. Randy had gone to high school with my cousins and didn't even know it. He eagerly produced the yearbooks. I opened to the senior class, and our search began.

We found David first. He was in the same graduating class with Randy. He appeared to have my dark hair and eyes. Next, we located David's younger sister Sue, in the sophomore class. She seemed to have blond hair. I resembled David more than Sue. So they were my first cousins. Seeing them increased my desire to meet Margaret. Randy got a big kick out of it. I thanked him. My vision of Margaret's family widened.

That night, my attention turned to meeting Margaret. I was looking forward to the visit but didn't know what to say. I'd read some examples, but none of them seemed exactly right. I sacrificed sleep that night and developed three sentences that fit the bill.

1. "Is Margaret home?"
2. "Do you have a sister named Nancy?"
3. "She is my birth mother, and I have the original birth certificate with me."

As I lost sleep, I lost count of the number of times those words echoed in my brain.

One thing was for sure. I would never forget them.

Once I knew where Margaret lived, driving by at least once a day became a regular activity. For the next six days, no one was home. Each time, I included a scenic trip to the store. There was a method to my madness. The more trips, the bigger my courage grew. Each time, I imagined walking to her door and ringing the bell. It was easy. No one was there.

First contact

The seventh day was different. A car was in the driveway. Someone was there. I couldn't believe what I saw and almost drove off the road. And in the process, six days of growing bravery had vanished.

I called Diana and let her know. She was ready for this new adventure. "Shall we go up to see Margaret?" I said, "I guess so." I had mixed feelings. I worried about Margaret's reaction to meeting me. Diana looked excited as she got into the car. I was glad she wanted to go. For the three miles to Margaret's, those three nocturnal sentences uncontrollably repeated in my brain. Turning back was not an option.

We arrived at 1:45 p.m., and I parked my car in the driveway next to the vehicle I'd seen earlier. My heart was pounding as I got out of our car clutching my birth certificate. Each step I took brought me closer to the new truths I would encounter.

I directly faced the door with Diana behind me. I rang the doorbell and heard footsteps from inside the house. What would happen? I held my breath. The door opened and from behind the screen, a tall, older woman appeared, dressed in a white blouse and blue slacks. Her kind, friendly face greeted me. She asked, "Can I help you?"

I took a deep breath while gathering my thoughts. I then started with the first of three phrases I had worked so hard to perfect.

Number one: "Is Margaret home?" She answered, "I'm Margaret." There's one.

Number two: "Do you have a sister named Nancy?" "Yes," she said. There's two.

And finally, number three: "She is my birth mother." There, it was done.

Wanting to show my earnestness, I simultaneously mentioned and pointed to the birth certificate in my hand. I continued by assuring her that this wasn't a scam. I was stopped in the middle of my sentence. This was it. What would she say? Margaret's words caught me by surprise. "I really felt that this day might come. Would you please come in?"

We walked in, once again with birth certificate being raised to eye level, while feeling the need to assure her of my honest intentions. Then another surprise: Margaret lovingly said, "I don't need to see it…You have your mother's eyes and mouth." None of this was going the way I thought it would. It wasn't what I expected. This moment was indescribable.

My initial concerns were now gently swept away. Those were being replaced by the feeling of acceptance. I instinctively hugged Margaret. By the way she responded, I knew this meant a great deal to her. She then hugged Diana as well. She motioned to us to sit and said, "My husband Jim is chasing a mole in the yard. I want him to come in and meet you." So far, so good. Margaret had been warmly receptive, but would he be as well? There was no time like the present to find out.

Jim walked in the door and said, "Hello," adding, "I'll be right back. I need to change out of my dirty clothes," all with a smile on his face. Why was he smiling? Before we knew it, Jim had returned, still in his dirty clothes, armed with a camera, and began taking pictures. What was going on? This definitely wasn't in any materials I'd ever read about reunions. I had no idea as to what would happen next.

I felt like a deer that had been caught in the headlights of a car in the middle of the night. While I sat there speechless, Jim put the camera down and seated himself next to Margaret. Diana was enjoying what she was witnessing, one of the few times that I was caught speechless. My old mental tapes began to play, "Why were they being so kind and friendly?" My worries of being accepted began to creep back in.

A burning question crossed my mind that needed to be asked, and I did so. "Did you know about me?" Margaret replied, "Yes. Everyone in the family was told shortly after you were born." Aha! This is why Margaret wasn't in shock when I came to her door, and why Jim smiled as he went to grab his camera. They knew about me! The usual scenario of the family not knowing about the adoptee had been reversed. They knew and I was the one in the dark. I didn't know about any of them. I definitely was the one who was more in shock at this point!

Then Margaret and Jim began to describe the type of person Nancy was. Margaret started out by saying, "I don't know how to describe her; she's a little bit different." I wasn't sure what that meant. As they continued, a picture of her personality started to form. She loved jazz and had sung with the top girls' choir in high school. Nancy was currently living in Vallejo, California. Then something I had always dreamed of became reality. "You have a half-brother, Tony." Margaret had no idea how excited I was.

When they were done describing Nancy, I felt it was time to ask another biggie. "Would she be open to contact from me?" Margaret didn't know. Jim thought that Nancy had wanted to put that part of her life behind her. I had heard that phrase before! I was becoming concerned about where this was leading. Margaret then said, "I never heard her say that!" She continued by saying, "She wasn't sure how Nancy would feel about all of this." I then told Margaret I was hoping that she would be our go-between to facilitate *contact**. What would be her reply? "Do you want to call her, or shall I?" Jim looked directly at Margaret when asking her this question. She replied, "Oh, I will."

Wait a minute…call who? Were they actually talking about calling Nancy? I couldn't believe my ears. I was reeling at this unexpected turn of events. Their conversation continued. Margaret and Jim agreed that Nancy was probably home. Margaret got out of her chair and walked toward the kitchen to use the phone. I was nervous, worried, and excited all at once. Would she answer the call? And what would Margaret say if she did? The mental script I had relied on was thrown into the trash.

"Hi, Nancy, this is Margaret. Are you sitting down? Your birth son is here." Margaret didn't mince words. She continued by telling Nancy that I was married, had four children, and was involved in music. Wow! I couldn't speak. As the conversation continued, Margaret walked into the living room, stopping next to me. Still talking, I heard her ask Nancy, "Would you like to speak with him?" I was astounded! Nancy must have said yes, because I was

---

* A common experience for many adoptees is that it can take weeks, months, and, many times, years to eventually have contact with the birth mother after first making contact with other family members.

handed the phone. It never occurred to me that I would be speaking to my birth mother just ten minutes after meeting Margaret. Now, I really was on the spot. What was I going to say?

"Hi, Nancy, how are you doin'?" (such a great opening line!) She said, "Fine." Then she asked me how I was. I said, "Fine, but nervous." She assured me that there was nothing to be nervous about. I managed to ask her how she felt about all of this. She said she was a bit shocked but glad that Margaret had made the call. She wanted to know if I had been well taken care of, and I assured her that I had been. She was very grateful for that.

I needed to have an important question answered and decided now was the time to ask it.

"Did you ever think about looking for me?" Her answer disappointed me at first. "No, I never did. I wanted to put that part of my life behind me." I then realized that this was the only way she could deal with the pain associated with surrendering a baby. The rest of the conversation was upbeat, punctuated with laughs, and ending with, "I'll talk with you later."

I handed the phone back to Margaret while I pondered the conversation that had just taken place. I had spoken with my birth mother! Margaret continued speaking with Nancy. A minute later, she ended the call and hung up the phone, saying that Nancy had left instructions. Margaret was to give me a big hug and kiss in behalf of Nancy. She did just that. I was realizing that Nancy would have kept me if it were possible. I was loved and wanted after all.

Before saying our good-byes, Margaret gently made me aware of two other things that had not crossed my radar. Worried that I would go away with the impression that the Blackstones were a "perfect" family, she told me that they had "warts." In other words, they weren't perfect. Great. I would fit right in. And the second was in the form of a question. "This makes me your aunt, doesn't it?" Since I had focused only on Nancy, I felt rather embarrassed.

Margaret was guiding me to the bigger picture. I apologetically replied, "I guess it does."

As we headed for the car, a feeling of total amazement washed over me. I had experienced what almost never happens to adoptees during their first attempt at contact. It went as well or better than I could have ever imagined.[†] Jim and Margaret had welcomed me with open hearts as well as arms. The reception I received emphasized the feeling of being family. The last thing Margaret said was "You are welcome to come back anytime you want." I could hardly wait for the next visit!

"Let's Meet!"

At home, I was still in a state of blissful shock. I pondered portions of my phone conversation with Nancy. Three of them would not go away: Nancy loved music, I had a half-brother Tony (I always wanted a brother), and we would meet. Nancy's love for me permeated the entire conversation of our first call.

Later that night, as I was preparing to go to bed, the phone rang. Diana answered, letting me know that Nancy was on the phone. I said, "Nancy who?" not yet grasping that it was my birth mother. She replied, "Nancy, your birth mother." I wasn't prepared to hear from her again so soon. As I was handed the phone, I couldn't help but wonder what she would say. I said, "Hello?" Her first words were, "Do you like jazz?"

Do I like jazz? Was that any way to respond to "Hello?" What the heck, Nancy was continuing a conversation that started at Margaret's. The next question was even crazier.

---

† The experience regarding my first contact with Margaret and Nancy was extremely positive, and does not represent all the 'first contact' experiences that adoptees encounter. It can take days, weeks, months, and sometimes years to finally meet for the first time. And in some cases, for a variety of reasons, contact never occurs. I was fortunate.

"Do you like kung fu movies?" Are you kidding? I responded, "I have seen some."

Still going on, she said, "You know that actor Jean Claude, Jean Claude…" She couldn't think of his last name. I completed it. "Jean-Claude VanDamme?" "Yeah, he's hot!" she exclaimed.

Was this really my birth mother? My adoptive mom was nothing like this. Why was she saying these things? Then it dawned on me. She was trying to connect by bringing up subjects that might be of interest to me. I had never experienced anything like this with my adoptive parents. Can this kind of conversation really take place between parent and child?!

"I have called all my friends, and they are so happy for me…" As she continued, I realized that Nancy was expecting our conversation to continue without a "good-bye" every time we spoke from then on. And on it went. We concluded the call by discussing a date to meet. She suggested Christmas, to which I initially agreed. However, this wasn't soon enough for me. I made a counter proposal. "How about March, during Spring Vacation?" She enthusiastically agreed. I then offered to travel to her home in Vallejo, California. "That would be just fine!" she responded.

As soon as I was off the phone, I let Diana in on our conversation. She felt that this would be the best way to facilitate our initial physical contact. Our youngest son, David, who lived at home, was asked about going with us. "Sure," he said. He wanted to meet the woman who had given birth to his father! Everything pertaining to our first meeting had fallen into place. The only downside to all of this was I had to wait two-and-a-half months!

I was back to visit Margaret on January 10. Since Diana wasn't available to go, I decided to go it alone. Feeling comfortable with the idea, I got in the car and traveled the three miles to her home. I knew the way blindfolded. The walk to her front door was much less stressful this time. I rang the doorbell, was greeted by Margaret, and welcomed in. Jim was seated in a chair, reading the paper. As fantastic as our first visit went, I was still wondering…Had their warm welcome been for real, or was it a one-time thing? I had to know.

After "Hellos" and hugs, I asked the question. Were they okay with everything? Jim and Margaret assured me that they were just fine, and not to worry. I was relieved. There was no need to pinch myself after all! Since I knew about Nancy's musical tastes, I was dying to find out what Margaret's preferences were. She started by telling me that she had played the cello in high school. I had no idea. Next, I learned that our taste in music was quite similar. Classical, choral, instrumental, and some country, as long as it was "good." I was then informed that Jim was not a musician and couldn't carry a tune in a bucket! He was an engineer who appreciated music in general.

Margaret had me follow her to their dining table. On it were some photo albums placed out conveniently for me to get to know the family. Once again, Margaret was acting as an intermediary. This time, it was visual. Included were pictures of my grandparents, Percy and Audrey Blackstone, Margaret, Tom, and Nancy as kids, and family members gathered outside of the church where Audrey's funeral had taken place in 1992. Nancy and Tony were part of the last picture, but too small to see in detail.

She then turned my attention to something that caught me by surprise. Margaret said that after Nancy had given birth to me, she and Jim had gone to visit her at Emanuel hospital. I was in rapt attention. I could almost hear what was coming next. "I got to hold you while we were there." I felt the love in her voice. "Holding you was a special moment." Margaret explained that as she held me, feelings of love and attachment were beginning to form. She realized they had to be locked away because of the pending adoption. No wonder our first meeting meant so much to her. She now was reconnected with the child that she never expected to see again.

Before I left for home, Margaret gave me something special to take—a handwritten list of information on the family, complete with names, birth dates, addresses, and phone numbers. I wasn't expecting this. Apparently, I had earned her trust. It was also another way of showing that I was part of the family. I was honored. Before we parted company, the all-important hugs were there. My feeling of being family continued to grow.

Nancy and I continued making plans for the first visit. We took turns phoning each other to iron out the details. I don't think that a day went by without speaking with Nancy. One concern centered around Tony. I had no idea as to how he felt about having a brother. One time I asked Nancy, "How does Tony feel about all of this?" She gave me his response: "Mom, I am your son." I asked Nancy what that meant. She told me not to worry—everything would be all right. I wasn't so sure. Was I horning in on his territory?

My brother

Although our conversation ended on a positive note, Tony's words haunted me.

He knew of my existence and probably hadn't given much thought to it. Tony was faced with the fact his mother had another son whom he would be meeting in the near future. I realized the need to reach out to Tony. I picked up phone and dialed his number.

"Is Tony there?" A woman's voice answered. "Just a minute, I'll get him." It was now three weeks after first talking with Nancy. I was excited to have a brother, but concerned about his true feelings. This would be my first opportunity to hear him speak.

"Hello?" Tony answered with a very deep voice, which intrigued me. For some reason, I was expecting him to speak in a higher pitch. Maybe that had to do with being brothers. And because of my background in vocal music, the overall pitch of someone's voice catches my ear quickly. Okay, he definitely was a bass-baritone.

After taking a breath, I began the conversation by introducing myself. First on my list of priorities was to find out which name he preferred. When Margaret mentioned that I had a brother, she called him Tony, but said his official first name was Malcolm. He had been named after Nancy's first husband. I believe it was changed because Nancy wanted to put the relationship behind her, including his name. Malcolm's middle name was Anthony, and that's where Tony came from. So I asked which name he preferred.

"Malcolm, but the family calls me Tony," was his response. Good. I decided to address him as Malcolm from that point on. Now that the name issue had been settled, it was time to change the subject. I began. "I want to let you know that I had no intention of hurting you when I first contacted Nancy." He was, after all, her son and I had burst onto the scene. I assured him that my intentions were honorable and I had the highest respect for him. I had given this my best shot. What would Malcolm's reaction be?

"Let me be perfectly frank. I'm cool with everything. And if Mom is happy, then I am too." Malcolm's voice sounded less reserved. As he spoke, I was beginning to feel at ease. Malcolm ended by reassuring me that, "It was all good." Even so, I wondered, Is that how he really felt?

"What have you got in your garage?" I had just arrived at Jim and Margaret's house for another visit. It was the end of January, and Jim appeared to be busy looking for something. Next to him was the centerpiece. A vintage automobile was parked there.

Jim proudly announced, "You are looking at a 1951 Packard." By the looks of things, it was a restoration in progress. He obviously enjoyed working on it. I couldn't remember the last time I'd laid eyes on one of those. Jim was an engineer by trade and loved tinkering on anything mechanical, especially his Packard! This brought back memories of my adoptive father. He had been an engineer as well. He had passed away twenty years earlier, and my recollection of him was very vague. My adoptive father had seemed like a nice guy, but we never connected as father and son, or ever got to know each other.

By contrast, there was a connection with Jim each time we were together. He always let me know I was wanted. He'd have probably let me change the oil if I'd asked! Margaret came out to the garage and told me she had just gotten off of the phone with Nancy (talk about timing). I said I would call Nancy later. Margaret and I talked a bit longer and topped off the visit with a couple of hugs. I knew in my heart that the acceptance and love Jim and Margaret had shown me was real.

I FIT IN

Boy, was I surprised! Margaret called and told me that she had scheduled a get-together with her family during the first week of March. She really wanted her family to meet mine. And besides, it gave her an opportunity to meet my family for the first time as well. What a great idea! I had been trying to think of a way to make this happen. Margaret must have been a skilled mind reader and beat me to the punch.

The day came for the families to meet. By now, knocking on Margaret's door was a piece of cake. Diana and our children, Denise, Danelle, and David, were there, except our oldest son, Doug. He and his family lived out of state, and so he couldn't attend. The door opened, and Margaret greeted us with a big smile. "Don and Diana, I would like to introduce you to our family!" I could tell by the way we were announced that she was excited. Jim and Margaret had set the stage for an enjoyable time.

Margaret got the ball rolling the minute we walked in the door. There they were, waiting for us in a semicircle. It resembled a receiving line at a wedding reception. Only this time, they received my family into theirs. My cousins Sue, Bruce, Cathy, and spouses were present, along with most of their children. Missing were Jim and Margaret's oldest son, David, his wife Cindy and their children.

I studied the facial features of each as individual introductions were made. The look of welcome and family resemblance reflected back, along with a hug or hearty handshake. Smiles and laughter accompanied all of this, which was music to my Blackstone ears. They were genuinely happy to meet us.

"Dad, you really fit in with this family!" That observation was voiced by my family as they watched me interact with all my new cousins. I felt an instant bond with each the minute we met. Everyone was so warm and accepting. The feeling of belonging washed over me. As we hugged good-bye, I realized that as the conversations would fade from my memory with time, their acceptance would always be foremost in my thoughts.

MARCH 2001—FACE-TO-FACE

"Are we all ready to go?" Spring vacation had finally arrived, and Diana, David, our youngest son, and I headed to California. The time had come to meet Nancy, Malcolm, and his wife, Vicky. We had communicated by phone more times than I could count to prepare for this experience. The last time I had crossed the state line south was on a family trip to Disneyland in 1970. I enjoyed Disneyland. This trip to the Golden State had a completely different purpose: meeting Nancy face-to-face.

No adoptee is ever fully prepared. Nine hours of driving gave me needed time to reflect. So far, the reunion had gone well. Margaret was the perfect choice to have had first contact with. She made sure I felt loved by showing family pictures, arranging for a get-together with her family, and letting me know that I was welcome in her home anytime. As we travelled south, I wondered if Nancy and Malcolm would accept me as readily as Margaret had. Keeping my expectations in check was a real challenge.

We made it! I just passed the Vallejo city limits sign. Next, we found the motel. Our lodgings were about two miles away from Nancy's address. I called to let her know we were in town. She excitedly made sure we had the right directions. I assured her we did. Nancy told me she would have a way for us to find her when we arrived. I could only wonder what that might be.

After checking into our motel, we accurately followed Nancy's instructions. Finally, I turned onto the street where she lived. It was 9:30 p.m., and my emotions were running high. I slowly drove down the street. Now I had to find her house. The street was dimly lit, making it almost impossible to see the house numbers. Where was her house? Or was it a house? There were apartments intermingled with homes. The emotion I felt turned into frustration. After driving up and down the street a couple of times, I told Diana and David I was going to park the car and begin a search on foot. Where was she?

I forgot that Nancy had a way for me to find her when I got to her street. If she did have, now would be a great time to reveal it. As I opened the car door and began to search, a jazz recording was playing loudly! Everyone in the neighborhood must have heard it as well. I turned to my left and spotted light coming from an open door on a second-floor apartment just above our parked car. That had to be her apartment. Who else was playing a jazz recording loudly at that time of night? Only Nancy!

My heart was beating loudly as we approached the screen door. I peered in. There was Nancy, seated in a chair, waiting for us to arrive. As soon as she saw us, she grinned from ear to ear! Nancy got up, came to the door, opened the screen, handed me Kleenex, and we hugged. Finally, we were together, face-to-face. I quickly scanned her features. Margaret had shown me a variety of pictures featuring Nancy, the last one dating from 1992. The majority of them were from 1975 or earlier. There were changes in her appearance, but I definitely could tell it was Nancy.

Nancy looked at me. She had expected to see me in tears, but I wasn't crying. Sounding a bit disappointed, she complained, "I bought this box of Kleenex just for you, and you're not even using it!" I could tell she was being funny. We all had a good laugh. If there was any ice to break, the Kleenex comment definitely did the trick.

Nancy invited us to sit down. She had waited for this moment ever since she was nineteen—her age when I was surrendered for adoption. I could only imagine what her thoughts and feelings consisted of. She looked at David. He was the first of her grandchildren to have seen or hugged. We talked about our trip from Portland to Vallejo and Margaret's role in all of this. She was glad that her sister had helped make this moment possible.

Just minutes into our visit, Nancy asked, "Would you like to meet Tony?" (She definitely called him Tony instead of Malcolm.) I blurted out "Yes." That was fast! I had planned to ask about Malcolm a little later, but she beat me to it. "When and where were you planning for our get-together?" She said, "You can meet him right now. He lives in the apartment next door." What? Another surprise—a huge surprise. But that was Nancy. Actually, I shouldn't have been surprised at all. It was in league with the other experiences related to my reunion thus far.

Out Nancy's door we went and twenty feet later, I knocked on his. The door opened.

"How 'ya doin' man?" I was staring at Malcolm's six-feet-three frame and a big smile. As we hugged, I realized how much bigger Malcolm was. "Little Brother" applied perfectly to me. He invited us in, and we were introduced to his wife, Vicky, her sister, and husband. This all was happening so quickly—everyone was welcoming us with open arms. Was this real? It was. I needed time to process the emotional overload.

For the next three days, Nancy, Malcolm, and I talked and talked—playing catch up on all the years we had missed. The day after our arrival we all went out to eat at a seafood restaurant overlooking San Pablo bay in the direction of San Francisco. Malcolm's wife, Vicky, joined us as well. The view, food, and company were terrific. Malcolm. Vicky and I loved Dungeness crab and ordered the same meal. Nancy, Diana, and David ordered fish and chips.

After ordering our food, Malcolm and I launched back into the conversation started earlier that morning. As we continued to compare childhoods, I was beginning to realize the differences. After Nancy had given birth to me, she remained in Portland, getting a job at the Multnomah Hotel located downtown. She liked going to the nightclubs playing jazz in northeast Portland. It was in one of them that she met her first husband, Malcolm, who played drums for different groups performing there.

After my brother Malcolm was born, Nancy divorced her husband and eventually moved to the Los Angeles area. Life wasn't easy for Malcolm. By contrast, I was raised in an upper-middle-class neighborhood in southwest Portland. At this point, I was tying into thoughts about how different life would have been if Nancy had kept me. I'll never know for sure.

In the meantime, Diana had gotten her camera out and captured our dining experience on film. I was totally oblivious to anything outside of the words we were sharing. There we were, my mother, brother, and me, talking and eating seafood together. Normally, pictures taken during a meal aren't the most photogenic, but the ones Diana was taking would be priceless. Nancy, who didn't normally like to have her picture taken, allowed Diana to shoot away during our entire visit.

Malcolm had membership at Gold's Gym and took David and me along as his guests. When we arrived, it was necessary for us to sign the visitor registry. Just after doing so, Malcolm called out, "Hey, man, come over here, and meet my brother," to a guy across the room. He came over and shook Malcolm's hand as well as ours. Malcolm had said "my brother." Wow...Those words were the greatest I'd heard that entire day!

I flashed back to my concerns with Malcolm. What were his thoughts about all of this? Malcolm knew I existed, but only as his mother's other child. My appearance changed that scenario. Before, he was the only child. Now Malcolm was the younger brother. As we spent time together, I got the feeling that he had made emotional adjustments before we had arrived for our visit. After Gold's Gym, I was put at ease.

Grabbing some ribs for lunch, we headed back to Nancy's apartment. From there, Diana and David joined us as we headed to Fisherman's Wharf at Pier 38 in San Francisco. Nancy had decided not to go. Malcolm and I continued our conversation—trading stories about how we grew up and our service in the military. I am quite sure that Diana and David felt like tag-a-longs. Vicky and her family in the area had planned a get-together that evening with Nancy, Diana, David, and me as the guests of honor.

We arrived at Vicky's sister's home in Vallejo at 6:30 p.m. We walked into the home packed with people—at least twenty-five. Once again, this reminded me of meeting Margaret's family for the first time. Rather than a semicircle as was the case at Margaret's, everyone here was in a large group. Each person I was introduced to welcomed me with a hug. I must have heard "How's it goin', man?" at least fifteen times. Vicky and I had a chance to talk. "I am so glad that Malcolm has a brother in his life." Then she shared an earlier conversation that took place with Malcolm. He had asked for her opinion about his new brother. Vicky said, "What's not to like about him?" She was solidly in my corner.

The next day, we said our last words, shared some hugs, and headed for Portland. The trip had been a success. I felt we had crammed as much talking and activities as possible in the time we had. Once we were home again, I had a chance to reflect. Our time together had gone as well as one could hope for. It reminded me of the "reality TV reunions" without the cameras, commercials, and audience: this was reality! Both Nancy and Malcolm had made us feel like family. We *were* family.

A LONG-AWAITED BIRTHDAY

My fiftieth birthday was coming up, and I had invited friends and family, including Margaret and her daughters to attend. At the time the party was to begin, Margaret and her daughters, Sue and Cathy, knocked on the door. We greeted each other, and I quipped, "It's about time that you made it to one of my birthday parties!" We laughed. I took great pride in introducing them to family and friends in attendance. Earlier, I had excitedly informed everyone else attending about successfully finding Nancy with the assistance of Margaret. Once again, I felt their love and acceptance.

The high point of this gathering was one I will never forget. Margaret was standing next to me as I opened cards and gifts. I came to the card from Margaret. I wondered what kind of card she might have gotten for me. She watched in anticipation as I opened the envelope. After reading the front, I opened the card. Staring at me were fifty one-dollar bills in a nice stack! Before I could say the words "Thank you," Margaret had an explanation for the amount of the gift. "The fifty one-dollar bills are for each birthday I have missed." I was deeply touched, and it seemed that Margaret received closure regarding the baby that she held fifty years earlier. Everyone there seemed to enjoy meeting my "new" relatives. It was a satisfying feeling.

Summer found me on a plane to San Francisco for my next visit. This time, I would be meeting and staying with Nancy's brother Tom, and his wife, Mary Bell, in Santa Rosa, California. I had seen pictures of Tom at Margaret's, so I had an idea of what he would look like. The minute I laid eyes on him, I couldn't believe how much he resembled my son David. It was uncanny. Both Tom and Mary Bell quickly made me feel welcome in their home.

Tom was seventeen when I was born. Compared to the uncles in my adopted family, he seemed more like an older brother. Professionally, he had been a teacher for thirty years before retiring. When I thought about it, almost the entire Blackstone family were teachers as well. Genetics!

I had a chance to talk with Tom about how he felt regarding Nancy's pregnancy. At the time, he was a junior in high school and involved in athletics. He would get teased about his sister "getting knocked up." Tom was really angry with her at the time. His reaction, though understandable, made me take a step back emotionally. Was he still upset about it?

"How do you feel about everything now?" I asked guardedly. "We really are glad that you found us. You are a great addition to the family." Boy, was I relieved! Since Tom lived in wine country, I was taken on a tour of the area, including the author Jack London's homestead. I was amazed at the number of vineyards in the area. With the sunny weather, it was picture perfect.

I spent one night at Nancy's. Her spare bedroom was mine each time I would come to visit. That evening, when Malcolm had dropped in to talk, we reverted to the mischievous brothers we never got a chance to be as kids and began to tease Nancy. She kept a water bottle with a spray attachment by her chair, in case she needed to cool off on a warm day. As we continued to tease her, she grabbed the bottle and declared, "Boy, I'm glad I never had to raise both of you at the same time!" and proceeded to spray away in our direction without ever hitting her targets.

AND THE BIRTH FATHER IS...

Nancy made her first trip to Oregon since reuniting with me in the summer of 2001. While here, we visited Virginia, a close friend and classmate of hers from her Corvallis High School days. Nancy thought Virginia would be our best hope when it came to remembering who she was dating at that time. On the way to Corvallis, the conversation Nancy started during our first phone call was still going on. It was her way of keeping connected.

When we arrived, Virginia invited us in. I had seen her in the picture of the girl's vocal group that Nancy was in. It had been some time since the two had been together, and they quickly began catching up with each other. Soon the conversation changed to who Nancy had been dating. I let her take the lead on this and Nancy got right to the point. She asked Virginia if she remembered the names of any of the guys she had gone out with. Virginia replied, "Honey, I wasn't really around during that summer, and we had lost touch with each other."

That was her answer? I couldn't believe what I was hearing. I began to wonder if they had made a pact never to reveal the birth father's name. By the time we left Virginia's, I was no closer to knowing who the father was than when we arrived. No names remembered. I was really disappointed! As we were driving back to Portland, I couldn't help feeling that someone besides Nancy should know, but who?

After that, conversations about the name of the birth father became less frequent. Pressing Nancy too hard was out of the question. I was worried it would jeopardize the relationship we had established. My adoptive mother's voice still haunted me. "And we can take you back anytime we want to" from my early childhood held me back.

After that, a yearly visit to Nancy and Malcolm became a regular part of my itinerary with each trip south. Over the months and years, my relationship with the Blackstone family had grown ever closer. They became the extended family I'd always wanted.

LOSING NANCY

In 2006, Nancy's health began to fail. That summer trip to visit her was to be the last time I would see her alive. She had been placed into an assisted living facility. I had made arrangements to meet Malcolm, Tom, and Mary Bell there. Nancy had been diagnosed with dementia. As we entered her room, the change in her health was obvious. The blank expression on her face said it all. She responded to conversations with a single "yes" or "no."

All of us had experienced Nancy's love for music. I wondered if she'd respond to it. Music was an effective tool in stimulating brain activity. I asked a staff member if they had a piano. He said one was in the dining area. Malcolm rolled her wheel chair in close proximity to the piano. While playing, I looked at Nancy. She had a smile on her face. For a few minutes, the old Nancy had returned visually and then returned to the blank look when I stopped playing. As we left, I had the feeling the end was near. Months later, I received word from Malcolm that she had passed away. She was seventy-five years of age.

Nancy had two memorial services—one in California, the other in Corvallis. My past experiences with family funerals made me feel like an outsider and not part of the family. Legally, I was not her son and expected the experience to be repeated. What transpired transformed me emotionally. Malcolm wanted my help planning the service in Corvallis. This caught me by surprise.

We went over the program order before the Corvallis service.

"Does that sound good to you?" he asked.

"Yeah, it looks great," I told him.

I supported him as his older brother. I never experienced this kind of inclusion before. During both services, my brother spoke very tenderly about the woman who gave birth to both of us. Through his tears, he shared the love a son has for his mother. I cried too, as my initiation into the feelings of love between parent and child took place. For the first time, I experienced loss of the mother I had grown to love. I truly missed her.

After the funerals, the one question that had been asked, but never answered, still remained. Who was my birth father? I had touched on this a number of times with Nancy. Her response was always "Honey, I just don't remember his name" followed with "and if I could remember, I'd tell you." She did say he had dark hair, dark eyes, and an olive complexion. He was part Native American. And if Nancy did remember his name, that information was buried with her. I reflected on how satisfying my reunion with Nancy and her family had been. The Blackstones had treated me with kindness, acceptance, and love. This was new to me and I embraced all of it. And as satisfying as this experience had been, a hunger to know the answer to the question still haunted me.

"You are so lucky!" friends told me. "You have a great (immediate) family, and not only were you able to find your birth mother, you got to know her as well."

"I totally agree with you." I would say. Then I would follow up with "but I really would like to know who my birth father is."

Most of the time, when I changed the conversation to finding my father, the others quickly changed the subject, or seemed to respond with half-hearted agreement. There was no way that they could possibly understand how I felt.

Diana and I decided to put a puzzle together one Christmas. It was an ambitious project, consisting of fifteen hundred pieces depicting a map of the British Isles. Two months after it began, it was still unfinished. England, Scotland, and Ireland had fit nicely together, as well as most of the water, complete with ships sailing and fish swimming.

Of the 1,500 pieces, 1,480 had been placed properly, leaving the remaining pieces to be figured out. For some reason, they just wouldn't go together. Then, I decided to count the number of remaining pieces. There were eighteen, and two were missing. Where were they? I had no idea. We spent days trying to locate those two pieces.

Every time I passed by the unfinished puzzle, where was my focus drawn? Not to the finished portion—I was drawn to the portion that was incomplete. There was a hole needing to be filled! I decided to check under the furniture nearby and what do you know? There they were, under one of the chairs!

Once I reunited the missing pieces with the others, the puzzle was completed in short order.

Once it was done, I realized that the puzzle quandary was very much akin to my father quandary. Some key pieces were missing, and I needed to look in just the right place to complete my birth father puzzle. Where would that place be?

The possibility of ever discovering the identity of my birth father seemed next to impossible. The hole where my paternal heritage should have been was dark and empty. Would I ever find the missing pieces?

WHO WAS MY BIRTH FATHER?

From the first time I asked Nancy for the name of my birth father and said she didn't remember, my desire to know continued to grow. "Hey, that's great that you found your birth mother. Did she tell you the name of the father?" I don't know how many times I'd heard that from friends after they had met Nancy during one of her trips to visit me. My window of opportunity was diminishing with every phone conversation and trip south to see Nancy. I realized time was slipping away.

Searching for my father became more frequent in my thinking. I was clueless as to my next step. By comparison, finding Nancy had been relatively easy. Her name had been on my birth certificate. And when it came to my birth father?

"The only information about your birth father was that he had been married and divorced. He had some Indian blood, but it was unknown how much, nor was there any reference as to what tribe."

Nancy had supplied this information. How accurate was it?

I had heard or read stories about adoptees receiving a copy of their original birth certificate that included the father's name, only to find out later the information was incorrect. For some reason, a false name was used. A one-night stand? A relationship not approved of by parents? A legal problem? An extramarital affair, perhaps? None of that mattered in my case. In this instance, I was lucky. Worrying about a false name wasn't an issue. The father's name was missing.

How much Native American was I? Could there be a way to find that out? I wondered.

In June 2006, I read about a DNA Y chromosome test that could determine the amount of Native American ethnicity passed paternally from father to son based on twelve markers. Results would reveal what general area of the world my paternal line originated from. The cost of the test was $245. That was quite a bit of money, but worth the investment. The only areas involving DNA testing I knew about were criminal cases and paternity testing involving blood samples. I called the testing company to find out what was involved. My curiosity focused on the ethnicity factor.

The person who answered my call explained the testing process and how long it would take to receive the results. Taking the test was simple. All I had to do was to open my mouth and gently scrape the inside of both cheeks with the swabs provided and mail it back. When the analysis was complete, I would receive the results in about seven days. After some discussion with Diana, I went ahead and ordered the test. It offered a simple and painless way to confirm my Native American heritage. For the next seven days, my eyes were fixed on our mailbox.

On the seventh day, I held the DNA test in my hands. Anxiously, I opened the box and carefully read the instructions. Taking the test seemed simple enough. I pulled out the swabs provided and gently scraped inside both cheeks. Upon completion, I placed them inside of the plastic bag provided, filled out the paperwork, and signed the release form. After a final review, everything went into the return envelope. As I drove to the Post Office, my thoughts centered on how much Native American coursed through my veins. In four weeks, I would have my answer.

FedEx delivered the results just shy of four weeks. My doorbell rang. I opened the door to a driver holding a stuffed envelope in his hands. Excitedly, I signed for the delivery and rushed to the kitchen. I could hardly wait to see the results. This time, there was no hesitation on my part as with my birth certificate. I was ready! I ripped the tab off the top, reached inside, and pulled out the paperwork. How much Native American was I?

I began reading the paragraph containing ethnicity. I suddenly stopped and went into shock and disbelief. I was almost entirely European, with a touch of Middle Eastern. *No* Native American! How could this be? My heart didn't believe what my eyes saw.

Had the testing company sent the wrong results by mistake? This just couldn't be right. I showed Diana, and she didn't know what to say. As I mulled this over for the rest of the day, shock and disbelief turned into anger. Accepting what I saw meant cutting ties with my birth father. Just thinking about the test results was painful. I came to a decision: No more DNA testing.

Without more information on my birth father, I was at a standstill. This part of my search was placed on a back rack in my brain. While I continued building relationships with Blackstone family members, the space in my heart for a paternal connection was empty.

It began on Halloween

October 31, 2013
The perfect time to look for a newer car was on Halloween. Diana and I decided to purchase a different vehicle. Trick-or-treating was happening that

evening, and we were the only customers. Every salesman working in the dealership was at our disposal.

We decided on the vehicle to buy, and the salesman went to get paperwork to close the deal. While he was gone, Diana talked about a genealogical program on TV. A man had taken a DNA test to confirm his Native American roots. "I recorded it just in case you might be interested in seeing it." She proactively recorded the program, just in case I agreed. She quickly added, "Great strides have been made in DNA testing since 2006."

I realized there was one more salesperson in the dealership that night. I was intrigued with the show's premise. "Okay, I'll watch it."

When we got home, we watched the show. The man featured was adopted and believed that Native American was in his DNA. As the story unfolded, I became hooked. It was my story as well. During the episode, he applied for and received a copy of his preadoption birth certificate. On it was the name of the birth mother. On the Internet, he discovered she had passed away.

He found a sibling and ended up meeting her. She told him that their father was Scottish and their maternal grandmother was Navajo. After meeting with a family genealogist, he was given names and a portion of their family history. He made a trip to the Scottish society in their state. The organization had put together a family tree that traced his Scottish heritage. He was given a kilt to put on and attempted playing the bagpipes.

As interesting as his Scottish heritage was, he still longed to confirm his Navajo link. He took a DNA test and waited a couple of weeks for the results. After they arrived, he gathered his family together to share the opening of the packet containing his answer. This was the moment he'd been waiting for.

Just before the end of the show, his results were revealed. His maternal grandmother was full Navajo, making him 25 percent Native American. He and his family were happy and excited. His belief became reality. My decision to never test again began to waiver. Now that I had been made aware of the advances in testing, receiving similar results for myself seemed possible. My heart reminded me of the empty paternal place longing to be filled.

Still wavering, I decided to sleep on it overnight. All during the morning, scenes from last night's program replayed in my head. Suddenly, the program stopped playing. I wanted another opinion. Needing to confirm my Native American heritage tipped the scales in favor of a second test. There was a proviso attached, however. If this new test failed to confirm my Native American heritage, I was done.

Diana had maintained an account with Ancestry.com for years. She had an extensive family tree and was dedicated to extending its branches. I, on the other hand, could have cared less about genealogy. The DNA division of Ancestry offered autosomal testing that both men and women could take. The results had a reach of up to eight generations. From what I had read, the results on ethnicity were a lot more specific geographically and you received a list of DNA "cousins" as well. The cost for the test was ninety-nine dollars plus postage! It was too good of a deal to pass up. I placed my order, and in four weeks, I would have an answer.

The second opinion

December 1, 2013
I was notified by Ancestry that the results were ready to be viewed online. Snail mail was history and anticipation filled me from head to toe. Finally, I would know how much Native American I possessed. After clicking on to my AncestryDNA homepage, I looked at the ethnicity section and my jaw hit the floor. I couldn't believe it—46 percent Irish, 33 percent Great Britain, 12 percent Scandinavian, with the remaining 9 percent made up of Western

European, Iberian Peninsula, Finnish/Russian, and Middle Eastern. I was out of numbers. Where was the Native American?

After being told by my adoptive parents, birth mother, and adoption agency that my father was part Native American, I had accepted that as fact from an early age. For the last thirty years, I had made a pilgrimage to the Warm Springs Indian Reservation in central Oregon annually. I camped next to the Warm Springs River, spent time with friends, and embraced my tribal roots. I was not in the mood to give up my trips to Warm Springs or my life-long heritage.

Something else courtesy of a discussion I'd had with Diana recently and my memory came back to haunt me. Years earlier our daughter Danelle had filled out paperwork in grade school, which asked for her ethnicity. She had listed Swedish and Native American! I'm sure there was some pride associated with that. Now that had changed. None of us had any idea!

Where was the Native American? I faced an ethnic dilemma. Believing the first test faulty, I had never considered receiving the same answer from a second as well. My problem was larger than life: How could I let go of my ethnic paternal connection?

That fragile bond with my birth father had vanished. I had nothing to hang on to. The word "adoptee" stared me in the face. It was time to face the truth. The belief in my Native American heritage had been based on incorrect information. I had been lied to. Why? Had the adoption agency made it up? Had Nancy guessed about the birth father's ethnicity? Or was Nancy involved with more than one man that summer? That would explain why she couldn't "remember" his name.

I was at a crossroads. Do I stop what I had started, turn my back, and cut my losses? I knew nothing and the thought of pressing forward into the unknown was almost overwhelming—would I ever find my birth father?

I was 46 percent Irish. Combined with Great Britain and Scandinavia, 92 percent of my DNA was Celtic. The only thing Celtic that came to mind was the nickname of a professional basketball team in Boston, Massachusetts. How would I emotionally handle my new ethnicity?

Becoming Irish

For two days, I pondered the evidence. Should I walk away from the whole thing and continue believing the lie, or should I acknowledge the truth and embark on a new adventure? In forty-eight hours, I had my answer. The past was the past. I accepted the results, embraced my Celtic roots, and made this commitment: no matter what it took, I would find my father.

Reality began to set in. Finding a needle in a haystack seemed almost easier than finding my father! I was open to trying almost anything if it would aid in identifying him. It felt like I took one step forward, and then two steps back. Would I have the patience and persistence that this journey required? My commitment meant there was no turning back.

December 9, 2013

What was my next step? In order to discover my paternal surname, I needed to order a Y chromosome test. My first experience with Y testing was the infamous one taken in 2006 that confirmed 0 percent Native American ethnicity. Deep down, that still bugged me. But the past *was* past. Eight years later, it was a different game as huge advances had been made in genetic genealogy. It was now possible to give a more detailed and precise analysis of the findings, along with a list of others that shared the Y chromosome with you. I was counting on it.

I became encouraged by the prospect. Since AncestryDNA offered a 46-marker Y test, I kept it simple by ordering this one from them as well. The advantages were obvious. Ancestry used the same saliva sample from my first test, which eliminated postage. The greatest part: the analysis began immediately.

JANUARY 10, 2014

I'd been waiting for it, but no longer—my Y results had arrived. As my eyes glanced over the page, there were noticeable differences from the autosomal test.

In the upper right hand corner, a rectangle contained information on my haplogroup. This was a new term to me. I had been designated L126, which meant I shared DNA with a pregenealogical group centered in the regions of Northern Ireland and Scotland. This entire group shared a common ancestor. That information was mildly interesting. I quickly moved on to the main attraction: the list of paternal surnames.

McWhirter, Boyd, Ferguson, McReynolds, McCullough. Those surnames were part of the list containing eighty-six names to be exact. I was excited to see so many. Almost the entire list had ties to Ireland or Scotland or both. Immediately, I had a starting point. For the first time, the ethnicity percentages from my autosomal test made sense. I was excited, that is until reality set in. Which surname was the right one?

I was a Celt with one goal and had no clue as to my next move.

I didn't know what to do with this new information. I knew there were a lot of surnames staring back at me with none close enough to be genealogically relevant. I read that only exact or very close matches would qualify. Based on a DNA relationship chart, the common ancestor I shared with my closest match would have lived eight hundred years ago.

I had become aware of two other testing companies, Family Tree DNA (FTDNA) and 23andMe. Both offered autosomal testing, just like the one I had started with at Ancestry. However, FTDNA had taken the lead in Y testing and would accept a transfer of my Y test data from Ancestry. I transferred my Y results, hoping to get a clearer picture of my paternal line.

JANUARY 11, 2014

I decided to order FTDNA's Family Finder autosomal test. Combined with the Ancestry test I'd already taken, my number of matches would double—so would the chances of finding my father. With autosomal testing, the overlapping segments of DNA are measured in units called centiMorgans, shared by you and your matches. I learned that every discovery made through DNA testing could be the one that causes a breakthrough in my search.

JANUARY 14, 2014

Jumping right into my new Irish heritage, I began acquiring books, clothing, and anything else that had ties to the emerald isle. Green had become my color of choice, especially when it came to socks and ties. As for Irish cuisine, I became a culinary expert in the art of making Irish stew and soda bread. My family was willing to vouch for that as they had become the beneficiaries of both delicacies more than once! Diana had been an active genealogist for years and had hoped one day I would get involved as well. Now that I had gone "Green" regarding father hunting, she might have wished for me to take up another activity!

My favorite place to shop for all things Irish was the Celtic Corner in Northeast Portland. On one of my frequent trips to the shop, Noel, the proprietor, told me about the All-Ireland Cultural Society of Oregon. He said it would be a good starting place for me to learn about the customs, culture, and music of the Emerald Isle. I thanked him for the suggestion. Since my goal was to become "Irish," I decided to attend one of their meetings.

Not sure if I was ready to attend a meeting by myself, I asked my son, Doug, to go along for moral support. Fortunately, he agreed. I had never gone to anything quite like this and didn't know what to expect. The meetings were held on the third Saturday night of each month. The next one was on Saturday.

When we arrived, I thought, "Here I am on another new adventure." What I found was a group of friendly people. Jim O'Connell, president of the club, was one of the first to greet us. He asked me my reason for attending. I told him the main reason that I had walked in the door was because of a DNA test. He was more than intrigued. The club secretary, Sheila Redman, asked the same question and got the same answer. After I was welcomed by a number of members, the meeting began.

This January's meeting was their "high tea," which only happened once a year. After everyone had a chance to sample the food and tea, Jim asked the visitors to introduce themselves. When it was my turn, I introduced Doug and myself and finished by telling everyone the same thing I had told Jim and Sheila—DNA testing, the Celtic Corner, and a need to know more about Irish culture had brought me to their meeting. Before the evening ended, several others had welcomed me also. I enjoyed my experience and became a member that night.

A MOVE WAS BREWING

JANUARY 21, 2014

I used the Internet to seek new ideas for my search. Irish Origenes located in Galway, Ireland, specialized in case studies based on Y chromosome results. According to the owner of the company, a finished case study could predict your family surname, along with a location in Ireland, Scotland, or England as a point of origin for your ancestors eight hundred to one thousand years ago. Test results led to a successful case study 85 percent of the time. The remaining 15 percent hadn't provided enough information to determine the surname and/or location. As an adoptee, would this methodology work in my case? If I qualified, this could expedite the discovery process significantly.

I contacted Tyrone Bowes, owner of Irish Origenes, and discussed the method he had developed. Right at the beginning of my e-mail, I asked the $64,000 question: "Would I qualify for a case study as an adoptee?" Tyrone responded, "Yes, It is possible, provided there is enough information to do the study with." That had a positive ring to it. Next, he explained the process. An analysis of my results was done at no charge or obligation. I agreed to the analysis. I was both intrigued and fascinated. He would notify me with his decision.

Three days later, I received Tyrone's answer. "Based on the results, I can proceed with a case study." I was overjoyed. Diana and I discussed Tyrone's proposal and agreed it would be worth the money. I quickly notified Tyrone of my decision to proceed.

The case study took about four weeks to complete. Tyrone sent weekly updates, partially to inform and partially to keep my interest going. They consisted of a list of qualified surnames based on his research. Each week, the list of surnames got smaller, while my excitement increased.

CROSSING THE WATER

JANUARY 23, 2014

"Oh my gosh, it's here!" was my reaction. The case study from Tyrone had arrived. What had he discovered? It felt like I was getting my birth certificate in the mail all over again. I stared at the message title for a moment and then decided to open it. While opening the e-mail, I was gearing up for shamrocks, shillelaghs, leprechauns, and more green ties. What crossed my eyes stopped me in my tracks: my homeland of origin was Scotland! The surname predicted was McCullough. McCullough made sense. There had been five McCullough matches listed on my Y37 test. Was my father Scottish?

Speaking of an unexpected turn of events, I had become so Irish that I had made plans for retiring to Dublin and opening a soda bread Shop! I had a green tie and sock collection to die for. My family and friends had seen and heard way more than their share about my Irishness—and now, to change ethnicity one more time? I had to face the music. I gently shared this new revelation with Diana and our children. Their response? "Dad, when you figure out who you are, let us know!" Upon my recant, my friends were good natured enough about the news, but I was thinking, now they know *I am* crazy.

Well, I mentally and emotionally packed my bags and soda bread shop and moved from Dublin to Belfast in Northern Ireland. From there, Scotland was in view and I would be able to keep one foot in each country. I wasn't ready to jump across the water into Scotland with both feet just yet. Time was needed to assimilate what I now knew. And what would the Irish Society have to say about my Scottishness? Once they knew the truth, I would be asked to never come back! My Y test results had produced surnames originating in both Scotland and Northern Ireland. I justified the Scottish tilt because of that. Should I start thinking about kilts?

FEBRUARY 23, 2014

Shortly after I received my case study, I was informed by Tyrone that he would be coming to Portland and Seattle in a week to present lectures on his case-study work. To my amazement, he was being sponsored by the Irish Society that I was a member of and the sister organization in Seattle, Washington. What were the odds of that happening? I excitedly made plans to attend the one in Portland.

Since I had six days to study my results in preparation for Tyrone's visit, I made a point of spending time each day studying them. The Portland Irish club planned to take Tyrone to dinner the night before the lecture. I asked Jim O'Connell, the Portland Society president, if I could join them. There was a method to my madness. This would be my chance to talk with Tyrone personally about the details related to my study before the lecture the next day. Jim's answer surprised me in a very good way. Not only was I given the green light to join them, but I was asked if I wouldn't mind picking Tyrone up from his hotel.

I jumped at the chance. It might be the only time I would have him all to myself. As soon as he was seated in my car, I introduced myself and quickly struck up a conversation involving his case-study work. Jim and his wife, Julie, joined in the conversation during dinner. At one point, I asked him how sure he was of his findings and especially mine. He looked straight at me and said with his Irish accent, "I stand behind every case study that I release." His earnestness reassured me. We wrapped up the topic as I transported him back to his hotel at the end of the evening.

Before leaving my car, Tyrone mentioned that he was having some hoarseness while speaking. As a vocal coach, I suggested having an herbal tea with lemon and honey at his side during tomorrow's lecture. As Tyrone got out of my car, he thanked me for the ride and, of course, the vocal remedy. Driving home, I reflected on the evening—getting to know Tyrone while having all my questions answered. This had been a once-in-a-lifetime experience.

The next morning, Diana and I arrived at Marylhurst University, where the lecture was being held. Many that attended the lecture were members of the Irish Club. Before it began, I approached Tyrone and asked if he had taken advantage of my tea recipe to help soothe his throat while he spoke. He nodded his head yes and thanked me, while pointing to a large cup next to the lectern. Tyrone took my advice after all.

Tyrone was introduced and without delay launched into an overview of Irish Origenes. As he continued explaining his theories and research, many in attendance looked bewildered. I, on the other hand, was enjoying the experience. The time spent asking questions the night before, combined with the preceding six days spent in review of my case study, had paid off. Tyrone's lecture added to what I'd already learned.

Leave it to the White Pages

March 10, 2014

I concocted a plan for my next move. I would create a form letter to send to every McCullough with an address in Western Oregon. It consisted of the following:

> *Dear _____,*
>
> *I recently found that I may be related to members of the McCullough/McCulloch family that lived in the Corvallis area during the 1940s and '50s. Some members of the family may still be living in the area. I found your name in the Corvallis white pages and wondered if your line of the McCullough/McCulloch family also lived in or around Corvallis during that time period. If so, I would really appreciate hearing from you. I am adopted, and am now searching for my father's family.*
>
> *My contact information is _____*

Receiving something by snail mail had its advantages. Many people would respond in kind when contacted in this fashion. I had thought of calling each one but soon dismissed that idea. Sending something written would give the recipient some time to think of what to say before responding. And I didn't want to chase a potential family member away by confronting them on the phone. When the dust had settled, eighty-four letters had been sent.

A SONG IN MY HEART

MARCH 17, 2014

It was St. Patrick's Day, and I planned to attend the Irish Society's annual event in North East Portland. I got a call from Jim O'Connell. He asked if I would sing the Irish National Anthem that evening, as the scheduled singer was ill. I was so surprised that Jim had asked me, the new Irish kid on the block! I said "Of course, I'd be happy to." It was an honor to be asked to perform the anthem of my new country of heritage. Then it dawned on me—I didn't really know this piece of music. What had I gotten myself into? I had only sung it twice with the members during club meetings, and that was it.

Realizing that everyone attending would know it better than I would, I hurriedly went to my PC and looked up the anthem on YouTube. I needed to hear a good rendition. Performing it well was important. And pronouncing Irish Gaelic—yikes! Finally, I found a suitable version from the opening of an Irish National Hurling match between Dublin and County Cork. What in the world was Hurling? It looked like LaCrosse, football, baseball, and rugby all rolled into one. I watched the craziness of what was happening on my screen. Learning more about Hurling had to wait. Learning the anthem was another matter.

I arrived at the event around 4:00 p.m., parked the car, and hoped for the best. As soon as the opening remarks had concluded the announcer said, "And now, the presentation of the Irish National Anthem." You could have heard a pin drop as I was given the cue to begin. When the last note was sung, I was relieved—I'd made it through! My performance was greeted with a warm applause. Several of the club members patted me on the back or hugged me saying, "You did a great job!" One of the long-time members was a bit more honest. He said, "You sang well, but your Irish needs some work." Before I could respond, he continued, "Actually, there are three major dialects of Irish, so no matter how well you'd pronounced the words, it still would have been incorrect, depending on your location!" Enough said.

The phone call for a memory

April 2, 2014

After thirteen years, I decided to contact Nancy's friend Virginia again. The first time was when Nancy and I had visited her. We hoped she might remember my birth father's name. We left empty handed. This time, I had a name to run by her: McCullough. She had been living in Corvallis, but had moved to Salem. A friend living in Salem had found her phone number for me. Would she remember our first visit? Would the surname jog her memory? I dialed her number.

Virginia answered. We took a moment to get reacquainted. I asked her if she remembered our last visit. She did. After some small talk, I asked, "Did Nancy go out with anyone having the last name of McCullough?" She took a moment, then said, "I don't know. That name doesn't sound familiar to me. As I said before, we weren't with each other during that summer [meaning 1950]." We spoke for a few more minutes and said our good-byes. I was convinced that Virginia either didn't know or had decided not to share that information, no matter what. I got the impression that this would be my last phone call to her. Another dead end.

The next day I reviewed what Margaret and Tom had told me. At the time of Nancy's pregnancy, Margaret and Jim were newly married and lived in Vancouver, Washington. Margaret was also pregnant with her first child. Tom was sixteen, a sophomore in high school, and heavily involved in athletics. He wasn't interested in Nancy's comings and goings, let alone whom she dated. Nancy was a free spirit and strong-willed. This worried her parents to no end.

She spent much of her time away from home. This made it almost impossible for anyone to have known anything. Who could shed some light on this mystery? Genetic genealogy looked like my only hope when it came to finding my father.

HOPE ON THE HORIZON

APRIL 4, 2014

Responses to the McCullough letters had arrived. Twenty out of eighty-four were in my possession. Of the twenty, twelve had been mailed, six were e-mailed, and two were by phone. Seventeen people had responded by saying that no one in their family had lived in Corvallis during the 1940s and 1950s. Two respondents made me chuckle: They wished me luck in my search, and let me know that they weren't the father!

One respondent named Alan left a phone message that intrigued me. He said that his parents had lived in Corvallis at that time and wanted to talk with me. He left his phone number and asked me to return the call. I was excited! Could I have stumbled on to my birth father?

APRIL 5, 2014

The next day, I was more than ready to dial Alan's number. When I made the call, a man answered. It was Alan and I immediately felt a connection. After I shared the scenario that included Nancy, he concluded that his father quite possibly could have been the guy.

At the end of his father's spring term, Alan and his mother left to live with her parents while his father Orval finished his degree during the summer term. Orval had lived alone at the time and quite possibly crossed paths with Nancy in some way. Alan and I came to the conclusion that he really could've been the guy. Could have been the guy? I was blown away! And even more astounding was the casual way in which Alan had agreed. Was there something he knew about his father that caused him to respond that way?

I then explained that DNA testing would give us the answer as to whether he was my half-brother or not. I asked Alan, "Would you be willing to take a DNA test? I would be happy to cover the cost." Alan responded, "I'll need some time to think it over."

His answer was more than fair. At least he didn't say no.

As part of our conversation, the subject of music was mentioned. Alan asked what I did for work. I told him I was a musician by profession. He said, "That's great. I have a concert on Saturday, and will be part of a duet performing a variety of music. I will be playing the flute, guitar, and singing baritone. Would you be interested in coming?"

A music performance? I was beginning to think we were already related. "Let me check my schedule, and I will get back to you." He gave me the time and location. Since he lived only a couple of hours away, getting there was easy.

Before our conversation ended, he told me something very interesting. The letter Alan received was addressed to his wife. She read the contents and learning it was for Alan, turned it over to him, rather than putting it into the round file. After reading the letter, he decided to contact me. I considered that to be a good omen. When I had hung up the phone, my brain went to work on the possibilities. Music genes were very likely passed down through DNA. Could his dad possibly be my father as well? My head was swimming, all at the expense of a good night's sleep.

APRIL 12, 2014

Diana and I had just returned from the concert. I learned that Alan and his colleague had been performing for a number of years. Before the concert began, he approached our seats and made a point of introducing himself. I had a chance to study his facial features up close. I wasn't noticing a lot of physical resemblances, but I was struck by his warm personality.

During the concert, I realized that Alan was a very versatile musician, performing on the flute, guitar, and singing baritone. The performance lasted for about an hour. While Alan was singing and playing, thoughts crossed my mind numerous times about the musical genes that we might share. Everything would hinge on the DNA test. But would he decide to take it?

When the performance was finished, Alan introduced us to his wife and invited us to lunch. I thought that was very generous of him, considering we had just met.

While we ate, Alan asked a lot of questions about DNA and what was involved in the testing process. I gave him an overview of everything involved (I still knew so little myself, but my salesmanship and enthusiasm made up the difference). I had given it my best shot.

After a pause in the conversation, Alan said that he would need some time to ponder our discussion. He wanted to do some research of his own before deciding whether or not to test. Alan assured me that I would receive a call as soon as his decision had been made. Alan's answer had been more than fair. He also seemed like a really nice guy who loved and appreciated music the way I did. The idea of Alan being my half-brother was growing on me, as were the possibilities of working together musically.

APRIL 15, 2014

An e-mail just arrived from Alan. What had he decided? Did he need more time to think about testing? I closed my eyes as I slowly opened it up. His answer was yes! He had decided to test—fantastic! I spoke to Alan later that day, thanking him for agreeing to test and letting him know when to expect the test to arrive. The results would prove whether or not we share the same father.

I quickly ordered the test from Ancestry after hanging up the phone. I estimated it would take another six to eight weeks for the results to be posted. As excited as I was, the length of time it would take to receive the answer tempered my mood.

I just finished watching *Philomena*, a movie featuring the story of an Irish woman in search of her birth son she had been forced to surrender many years earlier. It was recently released on DVD, and I had purchased a copy to watch at home. Soon after viewing it, I bought a copy of the book online. I quickly devoured it.

From the experiences the main character went though, it emphasized how time sensitive a journey of this kind was. The pivotal point in the story was when Philomena's son had been successfully identified, only to discover he'd passed away a number of years earlier. Such a tragedy! If only she'd started looking sooner. This applies to DNA testing as well. I didn't know my own life expectancy. Every minute counted while searching for my birth father.

APRIL 30, 2014

Alan notified me that he had received and taken the test on the 28th. Waiting for test results felt as though I was in slow motion. Being patient wasn't in my character. I was even learning to spell "waiting" in my sleep. I had the feeling that waiting would become a frequent companion throughout this experience.

Waiting for tests drove me crazy at times. One thing that helped keep my sanity intact was my employment. Performances for the community choir I directed, the Conchords Chorale were coming up. The remaining rehearsals gave my mind something other than Alan's test to think about.

A couple of days later, another response from a McCullough arrived. The man who called lived in a town near Corvallis. His family moved into the Corvallis area in the 1980s. He was thirty years too late. I thanked him for calling and crossed his name off the list. Alan's dad remained as the only possible candidate. One was better than none.

The learning cliffs

May 5, 2014

Within twenty-four hours, Alan had mailed the test in, which meant Ancestry would receive it a week later. The estimated date for results to appear was June 1. Was he my half-brother, or wasn't he? That was the question. Would I be fully prepared for either answer? I didn't think anyone was ever fully prepared, no matter the outcome.

As my Celtic roots began taking shape, the Native American myth I had embraced for so long gradually became a memory. Being Celtic came with a substantial learning cliff. I spent my spare time reading all things Irish and Scottish. I was familiar with each of the seven Celtic nations, including their origins. I had mastered a few key main courses of Irish cuisine and joined the Irish society. Actually, I had taken on two cliffs. The other was taking shape.

May 9, 2014

I attended the first day of the DNA class sponsored by the Genealogical Forum of Oregon. A month earlier, I had signed up for an online DNA class. My schedule and learning style weren't beneficial when it came to understanding the subject matter. Even though the lessons were well done, what worked best for me was a "live class" with other class members to interact with, along with an instructor on site.

The forum was known for genealogical information and had recently added DNA to its offerings. A class was scheduled twice a month on Wednesdays. Walking toward the building that housed the forum, I was really hoping that I would learn how DNA testing helped in the discovery process. I felt optimistic heading into the class.

A woman greeted me as I entered. I explained I was there to take the DNA class. She said the cost to take the class was seven dollars per session for nonmembers. But if I were a member of the forum, the class would be free. Once I had paid for the membership, she directed me to where the class was held. I located my class and found a seat.

Because I was early, I had a chance to scope out the other people attending. Most were female. There wasn't a young person in sight. Because everyone there was engaged in conversation, I had no way to tell which one was the instructor. A moment later, my question was answered. The person teaching the class introduced herself. "Hi, I'm Lisa McCullough."

McCullough? I couldn't believe what I had just heard. Tyrone Bowes had predicted this surname was mine. What were the chances of someone with the surname of McCullough taking the same DNA class, let alone teaching it? And most importantly, could we possibly be related?

Lisa began by asking each person to introduce him- or herself and spell out the reason for taking the class. When my turn came, I introduced myself and explained that I am adopted and searching for my birth father. I continued by sharing that both my Y test results and Tyrone Bowes of Irish Origenes suggested that my surname was McCullough. I finished with a flourish by commenting on my possible connection to her last name.

When the introductions had finished, Lisa asked to see my Y test results. She began going over my list of surname matches and stopped about half way down and exclaimed, "That's my first cousin!" Other class members who had been reading or talking with each other were now focused on Lisa's comment.

Her words had taken me back. I quickly put two and two together and realized that Lisa and I were related. I had just met my first paternal relative. Lisa let me know that we were most likely not close relatives. That brought me back to earth in short order.

MAY 16, 2014

Alan and I had been trading e-mails and pictures with each other in anticipation of the test results making their appearance. I was looking for any family resemblances—eyes, nose, mouth—although looks should never be counted on, DNA results never lie. Was I able to see any physical similarities?

The verdict was....possibly. One of Alan's brothers was a better candidate—hair color, head shape, and eyes matched mine to some degree. Again, we'd have to wait and see what the test results revealed. Even with similarities, I had to remain impartial until we knew. With our answer not far away, my hopes began to climb.

CAN YOU SAY "SQUARE ONE"?

MAY 21, 2014

Alan just called. He said that the results from his Ancestry test had arrived ten minutes earlier. "I've got some bad news. It looks like you aren't my brother," Alan stated somberly and added, "You don't appear as one of my matches." Could he be right?

My mind was reeling. I told him to hang on while I opened my AncestryDNA page to verify. If Alan wasn't showing at the top of my first page of matches, he would indeed be correct. As I looked over the first page, my eyes agreed. I admitted, "Yes, you are right. You're definitely not my half sibling."

"Oh my gosh!" was screaming in my mind. There was a moment of silence before either of us spoke. I broke the silence. "I was really looking forward to having a musician for a brother." "Me too," he said softly. We continued the conversation a bit longer and agreed to keep in touch. We still wanted to have a chance to make music together.

He was *not* my half-brother, and if we did share any DNA, it's less than the minimum that would've been recognized by the testing company. And his ethnic breakdown: 76 percent Western European, 10 percent British Isles, 4 percent Irish. We weren't even close to being similar ethnicity-wise.

Alan was the perfect fit when looking for a brother—a really nice guy with musical talent. And the circumstances seemed so right concerning his father, but there was no match. I could tell that Alan was disappointed as well. He had really grown to like the idea of having another brother, even if he already had four!

MAY 23, 2014

Two days after receiving the news, I really wondered about continuing my search. I was disappointed. Now I was also back to square one. Emotionally, I was drained. The challenge of starting over dominated my thinking.

I shared my feelings with Diana, Susan, Lisa, and others who knew of the recent developments. Everyone encouraged me to continue. Diana summed it all up beautifully. "Think of all the things you will learn as you continue to look for your father." That wasn't what I wanted to hear, but it definitely was the right thing for her to say. I had learned a very valuable lesson from Alan's DNA test—not to build up your hopes or ask anyone to test unless enough

DNA evidence and genealogical proof existed to justify it. Each test and the expectation that accompanies it were a financial and emotional investment.

Okay, what was my next move? Since I decided to start over, new ideas and increased DNA knowledge were essential. Then I remembered something. Nancy had told Margaret's granddaughter Carrie that she used to sing in some of the taverns around Corvallis. I found that in 1950, one had been owned by a family named Shannon. Now that's a good Irish name. Maybe that establishment was a meeting place for all the Celts in town. It was worth a shot.

A FLICKER OF LIGHT

Another trip to Corvallis was looming. Since Carrie lived there, I called and asked where I could find historical information that pertained to my search. She mentioned the Benton County Museum would be a good place to start. Located in Philomath, it was only a few miles west of Corvallis. I thanked her for the museum's phone number, and I knew what my next step was. Her idea had real potential.

I called the museum and inquired about any information relating to the history of Corvallis in the 1940s and 1950s. They transferred me to Mary Gallagher, the collections manager. She asked, "Can I help you?" I said, "Yes. I am doing family-history research, and I was wondering if you could help me."

After a quick explanation of what I was looking for, she said, "Of course!" She seemed friendly and enthusiastic about the project. We agreed on a date and time to meet. She might be a key person in my quest for a breakthrough. My enthusiasm was returning.

When talking to Mary. I had omitted the fact that I was adopted and looking for my birth father. For some reason, I worried that she might be put off and reluctant to help. The day finally arrived for my first trip to the museum. This might be the resource I had been looking for. As I traveled, my thoughts turned to all the areas I wanted to cover during my first appointment with Mary. When we met, I felt an instant connection. I soon found out why.

Mary asked what I was looking to find. I felt safe to disclose the entire reason for being there. Starting with my adoption, I shared details on reuniting with Nancy in 2001 and my ongoing search to find my birth father. I spoke of my disappointment connected to Alan's DNA test. I wrapped up with talking about the two possible surnames. I hadn't given up on McCullough and was expanding my search to cover the Shannon surname as well because of the tavern angle. That's where I wanted to start with Mary at the museum. I watched her facial expressions as I spoke. From my observation, she seemed fascinated with all aspects of the search. Would her verbal response correspond with her expressions?

As I finished, her response happily surprised me. "That's really cool. I was able to reunite with my birth family a few years ago. So, let's get to work and find your father!" Enthusiastically, I agreed. Mary understood what I was going through. So that was the reason we connected so quickly. How great was that? I couldn't get over it.

Mary immediately went to work and used the surnames McCullough and Shannon as references. In a short period of time, she found high school and college yearbooks, along with Corvallis phonebooks from the years 1948 to 1952 and brought them to where I was seated. She asked, "Is there anything else I can help you with?" I said, "No, thanks."

Mary excused herself to help another patron. I had more than enough to examine while she was gone.

I looked for listings with the name of Shannon. I found what I was looking for in the 1953 Corvallis phonebook. I tallied six Shannon families residing in Corvallis. And of that, two were connected with "The Peacock" tavern in the downtown area. Once I'd finished with the Shannons, I used the same process with the McCulloughs. Before leaving, I made copies of pages from the directories. I thanked Mary for her assistance and left for home. I had plenty of names, dates, and locations to process. I felt satisfaction knowing that much had been accomplished in a short amount of time.

The next day, I identified anyone named Shannon currently living in Western Oregon, courtesy of the online white pages, and mailed out another round of letters. I changed the surname headings from McCullough to Shannon. Simple. Would I have more or fewer responses to the Shannon letters than the McCulloughs?

May 26, 2014

Since Corvallis was a college town, I couldn't exclude the possibility that my birth father had attended Oregon State. My uncle Jim had gone there as well and possibly possessed a copy of the 1950 yearbook. If he did, I might stumble upon a picture and/or the name of my father. Jim had passed away in 2009, and Margaret subsequently had moved into an apartment. I called Bruce and asked if he knew where his father's yearbook might be. He said it was in the basement of his parents' home and made arrangements to get it to me.

As soon as I quit talking with Bruce, I finished addressing seventy-five letters to Shannons and took them to the post office. Another step completed. The Shannon letters had taken a lot less time to do than the McCulloughs. My system had become a model of efficiency. If another surname became a possible candidate, I was ready.

May 27, 2014

It was time to call the museum again. "Hi, is Mary Gallagher available?" She answered, and we made arrangements to meet on Saturday. Upon arriving,

Mary greeted me, and I was ushered to the usual spot in the library. The 1950 Corvallis phone directory was waiting for me. This time, I compared it to the surnames from the match list of my Y test and wrote down anyone listed with a matching name. By the time I had finished, a sizable number had been produced. My work was cut out for me.

Mary must have noticed I had an "unsure of my next step" look on my face. She took that cue and made a suggestion. "Have you thought about looking at marriage and divorce records in the county courthouse?" Mary remembered that according to nonidentifying information, my birth father had been married and divorced.

Checking records at the courthouse made perfect sense. "Thanks, Mary, that's a great idea!" I had a new direction to go. On the way back to Portland, I hatched a plan. Diana probably had experience going through records for genealogical purposes. I would ask if she was willing to help. This meant another trip to the courthouse.

MAY 30, 2014

The first response from the Shannon letters arrived. A woman living in central Oregon had called and left a message. She stated that her mother had worked at the Peacock Tavern, but had passed away a few years ago. She didn't remember her mother saying much about her experience while working there. Even if her mother was living, it sounded like she knew very little. That was the only response I received. Another dead end.

JUNE 4, 2014

I had just finished Lisa's third DNA class. She announced Ancestry had discontinued Y testing and would remove all existing test results from their site in the near future. I was really glad that I transferred my Y results to FTDNA. On her recommendation, I decided to upgrade to the 67 test. It would increase the chances of receiving a more definitive list of surnames. The possibility also existed that the 67 wouldn't reveal anything new, but I was willing to risk it. Lisa had an effective teaching style and kept us posted on new developments in the DNA arena. Another benefit—Lisa and I had become friends. I learned that it took a community of people working together to have a successful search. Today's class proved it.

JUNE 12, 2014

Ah, the process of elimination. It's a new procedure I was mastering. In this case, it pertained to the minimal amount of centiMorgans shared between matches to be considered meaningful relationship-wise. Lisa recommended no less than 10 cMs. Lower than that could represent DNA passed down by coincidence, or from a very distant ancestor. The bottom line: the more DNA you share with another match, the more likely you are to have a closer relationship.

KINDRED SPIRITS

JUNE 15, 2014

Diana and I just got back from the Newport Celtic Festival on the Oregon coast and enjoyed it immensely. I felt very much at home. All of the Celtic nations (Scotland, Ireland, Wales, Isle of Man, Brittany, Cornwall, and Galicia) were represented through the exhibits, cuisine, native apparel, highland games, march of the clans, music, dance, and of course, the haggis-eating competition.

Before the competition began, it was announced by the bagpipes. As the pipes played, the platter carrying the haggis was proudly paraded around the spectators at an extremely slow pace. Everyone had the chance to closely inspect and admire the guest of honor. I looked at Diana and asked her, "Would you like to try some?" "No, not really."

Just before the competition began, a man in a kilt standing next to me said, " I know which one is going to win," referring to the competitors. I said, "How do you know?" "The last man on the right is standing. He knows exactly what to do." Was he right?

I stood there, waiting to find out. The announcer said "Go," and the manly contestants began stuffing their mouths in a frenzy. When it was all over, he was right! There must have been a method to eating haggis.

As we toured the exhibits, I felt enveloped by my kinsmen and heritage. Each clan had a tent or exhibit space to display posters and brochures about their culture. I was envious of those who proudly shared the legacy of their clan and longed for the day when I would be able to do the same. Emotionally, I had spent the day window shopping for mine. If only McCullough had been the one.

I left the festival with a stronger bond to my Celtic roots and an increased desire to search for my paternal roots. As Diana and I traveled home, three realities stared me in the face. My Y-67 results hadn't arrived, I had no information to create a paternal family tree with, and I struggled with certain aspects of interpreting DNA test results. I needed more time and patience with each.

JUNE 19, 2014
Lisa just finished teaching my fourth DNA class. It was great being taught by a distant relative. The subject was "How to build a DNA family tree." All I had to work with was surnames from my Y test results. How in the heck did you know where to put them?

It made no sense. Lisa asked, "Are you confused?" I nodded my head affirmatively. She took pity on me and offered to help. Lisa asked for my Ancestry account access information and offered to come up with a plan for surname placement. After thanking Lisa, I told her about the Newport Festival and how it felt like "home." She smiled.

JUNE 20, 2014
A possible breakthrough occurred. Lisa informed me that three of my matches were related to her McCullough line. That sounded promising. I couldn't wait to see what she had found. How was she able to do that?

JUNE 27, 2014
Maybe I was "getting it" after all. Triangulation was a method by which a common ancestor could be found. It occurred when at least two of your DNA matches shared DNA with each other as well. If each of those matches had extensive family trees, the likelihood of identifying the common ancestor was increased. My problem? I hadn't run into that scenario yet. It was just a matter of time. Meanwhile, I had yet another reason to hone my skill in patience.

JULY 5, 2014
Two-thirds of my Y 67 test results just arrived by PC. The last third was missing. I became extremely frustrated. Without the entire set of markers, comparisons with other people's results was impossible. So close and yet so far. I was back to waiting once more.

JULY 8, 2014
During DNA class today, I realized that with Lisa's help it was all beginning to make sense. I was close to interpreting DNA test results on my own, which brought a smile to my face. Returning home, I logged into my FTDNA account. What greeted me was less than satisfactory. My remaining Y 67 results had been pushed back another two weeks. There went the smile. It was back to being patient and continuing to learn.

Building "The Wall"

JULY 12, 2014

It was time to build "The Wall." If I could convince as many members of Nancy's family as possible to do a DNA test, a wall of maternal DNA would form. I could then compare my matches to "The Wall." If they matched any or possibly all of my maternal family, they would be disqualified as a paternal match. If they didn't match anyone in "The Wall", I very likely was looking at someone on my paternal side.

I needed to contact members of the Blackstone family to get their approval. Tom and Carrie had already tested at Ancestry. My plan was to have them transfer their raw data to FTDNA. Everyone else would test there as well. When finished, "The Wall" would be an effective tool in separating paternal from maternal matches.

JULY 20, 2014

I began the day with a call to Malcolm. I explained the reason for having him take a DNA test. He simply said "No problem." I said the cost was covered and would send him the test after it arrived in my mailbox. I was off to a good start, but would everyone else be as agreeable?

The "Y" for understanding

JULY 31, 2014

I was still waiting for the remaining Y test markers. Where were they? I resigned myself to another period of waiting. After lunch, I went back to check one more time. Yes! In my absence, they had posted. With all sixty-seven markers in my possession, I had sixty-six matches. Surnames, such as Gillespie, Malone, Ferguson, Diamond, McGinnis, and McWhirter, appeared more than once. I was excited! Upon closer inspection, the excitement waned. My closest Y matches and I were sharing a common ancestor that lived six hundred to eight hundred years ago. I was still determined to make contact as e-mail addresses were included. I began with the closest multiple matches on my new list. I created a form letter that gave a short explanation for contacting them and included it with each message. How many would respond?

Within a day or two, I received seven replies. A Gillespie who responded said his cousin Connie McKenzie, the Gillespie Project administrator, would contact me. A day later, I received a message from Connie. She wanted to know how I was connected to the Gillespie surname.

After I explained about my adoption, DNA tests taken, and surname connections, she invited me to join the Gillespie Project in order for her to review my Y test results. In one DNA class, Lisa had advised anyone who had taken a Y test to sign up for applicable surname and geographical projects at FTDNA.

I received Connie's answer the next day. She determined I wasn't a close match to other project members, and more than likely not a Gillespie. At that moment, I stopped reading. Here it comes—I'm not accepted into the project. Adoptees feared rejection. I brushed off the negative and continued reading. She decided to adopt me into the project in order to help with my search. She wanted me to find my father!

In her next sentence, Connie asked if I was ready to work. I responded, "Absolutely!" Connie sent an outline of what needed to be done. First, I needed to upgrade to the 111 test, the highest standard one available. Because so many surnames appeared on my sixty-seven results, the upgrade was my best hope in narrowing down the list. And perhaps one would stand out as the obvious choice. I agreed with her reasoning and ordered the upgrade from FTDNA. Next, Connie sent reports and examples to increase my understanding about

Y testing. She wanted me to learn as much as possible, and in turn, know how to use the information. I concluded understanding DNA required a real commitment from the test taker: me.

A FORTRESS EMERGES

AUGUST 4, 2014

I went back and reviewed my autosomal results on Ancestry and FTDNA. Tom called and informed me that he ordered a Family Finder test to help build "The Wall." This had become the code name for my maternal family's DNA results. Tom was determined to help find my father as was the rest of the family. This reminded me to call the other Blackstones about taking the Family Finder test.

AUGUST 10, 2014

More and more fifth to eighth DNA cousins were appearing, while relatively few fourth cousins and closer were showing. This was a bit frustrating, but it made sense. Everyone had more distant cousins than closer ones. With each generation back, the number of direct ancestors doubled. I had no idea as to which matches were paternal. Maybe none had tested.

AUGUST 20, 2014

Lisa kept my DNA class interesting and informative. We learned about interpreting overlapping segments of DNA on individual chromosomes. The longer the overlap, the closer the match. And then we discussed something that made my ears perk up. Adoptees should test with all three companies (FTDNA, Ancestry, and 23andMe). Most people test with only one. I would miss out on comparing my results with the majority of test takers, so I decided to test with all three. More people were testing every day, which increased the likelihood of having a crucial match show up on your computer screen. In my case, the right people hadn't tested on the paternal side.

AUGUST 25, 2014

It happened! Malcolm's Family Finder results were in. The overlapping amount of DNA shared proved he was my half-brother! It was great to see DNA prove what I already had on paper. Malcolm and Tom were in place on "The Wall."

I called Margaret, Dave, Sue, Bruce, and Cathy asking them to test with FTDNA as well. Since Carrie had already tested at Ancestry, I asked her to transfer the raw data to FTDNA. When all of that was completed, "The Wall" would become a "fortress." I couldn't wait to start separating my matches— the maternal from the paternal.

IT HAPPENED IN HOUSTON

SEPTEMBER 6, 2014

Connie McKenzie had confidence in me. She continually fed me DNA articles to read and diagrams to study. Every so often, she threw me a Y DNA problem to solve or an opinion to render. This kept me extremely busy. Just when I thought there was a moment to pause and smell the roses, Connie would toss something new at me. Yikes! Deep down, I knew all of this would come in handy when the time was right.

SEPTEMBER 14, 2014

Connie threw a curve ball. She said that FTDNA was hosting the tenth annual Project Administrators Conference in Houston, Texas, from October 10 to 12. Connie had attended the conference in the past but was not able to make it this year. She felt strongly that I should go. In order to attend, I would need to be an administrator, or a guest of one. The solution was for Connie to add me as a coadministrator of the Gillespie Project.

Was I up for this? Sure, why not. The thought of attending the conference was exciting, even though I would probably be way over my head in the knowledge department. Nothing like a trial by fire. I told Connie I would talk this over with Diana and let her know what my decision would be. Given the opportunity to learn from some of the best in the field and expand my network of friends and mentors, the choice was obvious. Diana and I were going to Houston, Texas. Who knew?

SEPTEMBER 27, 2014

I started my countdown to Houston by registering for the conference online, along with making flight, car, and hotel accommodations. When that was accomplished, going to Houston became a reality. And thanks to Connie, I now was a coadministrator for the Gillespie Project. Next, I cranked up the learning process—read, reread, and reread again. I wanted to be as prepared as possible.

Emily Aulicino, author of *Genetic Genealogy: The Basics and Beyond,* was the speaker at the next DNA class I attended. Nationally recognized as one of the leading experts in DNA testing, it was our good fortune to have her residing in the Portland area. I was really looking forward to hearing what she would talk about. Before Emily spoke, I asked her to sign the copy of her book that I had purchased earlier. She happily complied.

Emily covered a number of DNA basics, including testing with each of the major companies. Her explanations were always quite detailed and interesting. And as usual, I picked up a couple of new tidbits to chew on. I was seriously considering writing a new song titled, "It never hurts to hear the basics one more time." After the class was over, I was thrilled to find out that both Emily and Lisa would be attending the conference in Houston as well. I would be in good company.

OCTOBER 1, 2014

I signed up again for the online DNA class that I hadn't finished four months earlier, which was offered by DNAAdoption.com. The first time I took it, I knew very little about DNA. Combined with my learning style, I was doomed to fail from the get go. My confidence had grown because of classes I had taken at the Genealogical Forum of Oregon, and of course, Lisa's hands-on teaching approach.

OCTOBER 2, 2014

23andMe was the third major company that offered autosomal testing. I had ordered a test from them as well. Testing with Ancestry, FTDNA, and 23andMe was crucial for me. Because many people choose only one company to test with, adoptees who test with all three have the greatest chance of matching a key birth family member. I wanted to make every match count.

OCTOBER 3, 2014

I had my first phone conversation with Connie McKenzie today, and I really enjoyed talking with her. The first thing we covered was the upcoming conference in Houston. She enthusiastically explained the overall picture of events, along with a description of the different sessions being offered. Next, she gave me a rundown on the presenters and their areas of expertise. Connie asked if we had our accommodations and flight booked. I assured her we did.

After our call ended, it dawned on me that Connie had mentioned working with Y DNA testing for over ten years. Me? A whole ten months. The comparison kept me humble. Connie emphasized the need for surname confirmation through Y testing more than once. In her mind, a close match at

111 markers was crucial. To emphasize that, Connie told me she would never be convinced unless the surname was associated with a close Y 111 match. This had become my mantra as well.

"I'm adopted"

OCTOBER 10–12, 2014
It was the first day of the conference, and we'd just arrived in Houston. The hotel we stayed at was also the site of this event. How convenient. That night, a "get to know you" affair was held, where attendees could meet and greet. The next day, after the welcoming remarks by some of FTDNA's leadership, sessions began in earnest. I had pen and paper handy and was ready to learn. I was glad to have made the decision to attend.

Aside from the lectures which were informative, three other experiences left a big impression on me. The first happened just before the first session. I had found a place to sit. Seated next to me was a woman from California who introduced herself and gave her reason for attending the conference: "I'm a professional genealogist from California who specializes in helping adoptees find their birth parents."

Did I just hear what I thought I heard? "Really," I responded. "I'm an adoptee from Portland, Oregon who wants to learn as much as possible about DNA testing to help in the search for my birth father." She turned her chair in my direction and began asking what I had done in my search, and was there anything she could do to help. I hadn't expected her to make an offer like that. I thanked her for the offer. Was that an omen of things to come?

The second experience happened during the break for lunch. FTDNA had provided the lunch for all attendees, and we were seated in groups of twelve at round tables. After we were seated, everyone introduced themselves and explained why they were attending. The person to my left was the first one to begin. As I listened to each person, I became a bit intimidated as their credentials were made known. It was very apparent who the rank amateur was. Then came my turn. "Hi, I'm Don Anderson from Portland, Oregon, and I'm an adoptee in search of my birth father."

All of a sudden, everyone began asking if I'd tried this or that, had I read certain articles, what tests I had done, and the suggestions and questions kept coming. Could someone have said "Feeding Frenzy?" I was overwhelmed— partially because of their knowledge and partially because of their desire to help. Before we left the table for the afternoon session, I thanked each of them for their advice and recommendations.

My third experience affected me the most. After Alan McCullough was proven not to be my half sibling, my confidence level had fallen. I had real concerns that my future efforts would yield nothing. And as the weeks went by, I found myself "white knuckling" more and more, just to keep going. I had heard that Richard Hill, author of *Finding Family—My Search for Roots and the Secrets in My DNA*, was attending the conference. I'd never heard of anyone who had been successful in this kind of endeavor up until I read Richard's book. I hoped to have a chance to speak with him. My opportunity presented itself during one of the breaks between sessions. I spotted him standing alone, walked toward him, and took advantage of the moment.

"Richard, I'm Don Anderson and I wanted to talk to you about your book." I shared an abbreviated version of my story and then asked him, "Did you really find your father through DNA testing?" As an adoptee I wanted his personal confirmation. What he said next made the biggest impact. "Yes, I really did. And if you keep moving forward, something good will come of it."

I knew the main reason for attending the conference: to meet and speak with Richard in person. My conversation with him had given me the hope and courage needed to keep moving forward.

We just got back from the conference in Houston. The good news: It was more than worth going to. My DNA batteries were charged and ready to go. My network of DNA mentors had increased, thanks to Emily's connections. I knew a fair amount about DNA before the conference. The reality: I learned that there was still much to learn.

Projects and paperwork

October 25, 2014

After I returned from Houston, joining FTDNA's projects was foremost on my mind. Most of the projects were centered around results from Y tests. Projects had been discussed during the conference. Projects were mainly classified by surname, location, and haplogroup. When joining, your results would be grouped with others showing similar results. I signed up for projects that represented multiple matches on my 111 test, as well as ones that were connected to Ireland and Scotland.

My list of DNA projects joined was growing. Besides the Gillespie Project, I added the Henry, McGinnis, and Ireland yDNA, to name a few. Once it was official, I contacted the administrators and shared a brief version of my story. Those who replied offered varying amounts of advice and information to further my search.

Margaret Jordan, coadministrator for the Ireland yDNA Project, took a special interest in my search. She reminded me of Connie McKenzie because of that. After looking over my Y results, she observed that I definitely belonged in her project. There wasn't anyone else that matched me closely enough to be genealogically relevant. Margaret made a commitment to contact me if a close match surfaced.

OCTOBER 30, 2014

A year had passed since Diana and I had a discussion about testing on Halloween. To celebrate, I reviewed the nonidentifying information on the father. It stated that he'd been married and divorced. Nancy very possibly named me Richard Allan to remember him by. Mary Gallagher had suggested going to the Benton County Courthouse and search birth, marriage, and divorce records from 1945 through 1952. There was a chance that the birth father had been named in one of those transactions. Because this task was labor intensive, I enlisted Diana's help. Since this wasn't something I looked forward to, it was definitely classified a labor of love. Oh boy, another trip to Corvallis!

NOVEMBER 3, 2014

There we were, in the basement of the Benton County courthouse, looking at records on microfilm and jotting down anyone with the names Richard or Allan. I realized this would be a time-consuming job, but hadn't expected the jumble we ran into.

All legal actions in Benton County had been recorded together, organized by date, rather than category. Yikes! Because of the way entries were organized, it was tiring to focus for long periods of time. Diana and I were there a lot longer than anticipated. We headed for home with handwritten copies extracted from the microfilm, "screen fatigue," and writer's cramp. It was unanimous: Neither of us wanted to repeat this adventure any time soon.

That evening, I sat down and studied each page for clues. It reminded me how much work had been done earlier that day. As I read each name, I realized there were a lot of Richards and Allans living in Benton County at that time. And to make matters worse, I had no idea as to when the marriage and/ or divorce had taken place. Were any of these my father? When I reached the bottom of the last page, I concluded this had been an exercise in futility.

November 5, 2014
Our son, Doug, came up with a brilliant idea. Create a Facebook page about Nancy—include pictures and her life story. Since the medium was used by millions of people, it was an effective way to connect with those who knew her. Would we get any nibbles? Time would tell. Would we receive any clues as to my father's identity? It was worth trying.

November 7, 2014
What had Nancy's activities consisted of when she was a teenager? I reviewed what various family members had told me. Two of them stuck out in my mind. Nancy had told Carrie a number of years ago that she had sung in the bars around Corvallis when she was eighteen and occasionally liked to "hop on" for a motorcycle ride. Both sounded like things Nancy would've done. My imagination was all over the place. The father could have been passing through Corvallis at the time, stopped for a drink, had a little fun, and left town. Or, maybe a student at OSU used a motorcycle to get around and happened to give Nancy a lift. Was there anyone living that witnessed any of this?

"Tell me about your father's side."

November 13, 2014
GEDmatch was a great resource for those who had done autosomal DNA testing. It allowed anyone who had tested with FTDNA, Ancestry, and 23andMe to upload their data from the testing company to GEDmatch and compare their results with anyone else who had done the same. Each person who used GEDmatch usually had contact information attached.

That is where Robert Liguori came into the picture. He came to a brick wall on his maternal line and had sent out e-mails to each of his fourth to sixth cousin matches. I was contacted, as we were estimated to be fifth cousins on

FTDNA and GEDmatch. I initially determined that he was a paternal match. When I compared him to Malcolm, no DNA was shared. I let Robert know that he seemed to match my paternal side. Had I found my first paternal relative?

"'Do you know a T.B. on Ancestry?" Looking quickly, I replied, "Yes, that's my uncle. Why?"

I was disappointed by Robert's returned message. "Your uncle matches my mom and I."

My paternal balloon just got popped. Now, both Robert and I faced brick walls. My experience with a likely dead end meant contact usually stopped. The match would go on to something easier. That would be the last I'd hear from Robert.

To my surprise, another e-mail from Robert was waiting for me to open the next morning, Had he found another connection? "Can you tell me about your father's side?"

Rather than attempt an e-mail, I asked if we could talk over the phone, as there was too much detail for an e-mail. He readily agreed and gave me his number.

I quickly dialed and he answered just as fast. I told him I was adopted, had found my birth mother in 2001, and was never told the name of my father. Because of that, I had been using DNA testing to find him. I must have said the right thing, because Robert exclaimed, "We need to find your father!" The phone almost jumped out of my hand.

"What have you done so far?" I started with my first Ancestry test and concluded with his initial e-mail. "That's everything."

"I'll see what I can dig up. We'll be talking soon."

Over many phone calls the next couple of days, Robert put together a plan organizing our efforts. Part of that plan was to allow him access to my Ancestry account. He helped contact my matches that had McCullough, Shannon, and others of Irish/Scottish origin. Any match contacted had to share a minimum of 10 centiMorgans. I thanked Robert for putting a plan in place. I couldn't help but wonder—how long was Robert going to stick with this?

NOVEMBER 15, 2014

Robert reenergized my search. I resumed efforts to build "The Wall" as big as possible. I wondered how many maternal family members would actually test. I went over my list. Tom, Malcolm, and Carrie had all taken one. Now if Margaret, Dave, Sue, Bruce, and Cathy agreed to do the same, my wall would be pretty impressive. If someone was a maternal match, the chances are that they would match at least one of the eight.

Robert continued to be on my DNA trail. He found a match that looked promising. This individual matched me on both Ancestry and FTDNA family Finder, but didn't show as a match with any maternal family members at either company. I had contacted the match, and after searching, couldn't find a common surname between my Y matches and the ones on his family tree. I began to realize that without having a confirmed paternal surname, the search would be very challenging and take longer than expected.

NOVEMBER 18, 2014

I was still attending Lisa's DNA class at the Genealogical Forum of Oregon. Much of what she was covering I had heard more than once. Repetition never hurt when it came to learning about DNA. In my case, it usually took a number of times to understand its aspects. But one thing had always haunted my thoughts—I felt like a genealogical "window shopper." I was always looking through the glass at the hundreds of surnames posted, and wouldn't have the information to select the right one. Which one was mine?

One more time around...

November 22, 2014

Something was eating me. After I received the news that Alan McCullough was not my half-brother, I initially accepted the answer. DNA tests didn't lie. But the thought kept nagging me—Could it be possible that Alan's father Orval might be mine, but for some reason, Alan and I weren't a match? The only way I could know for sure was to have his dad test as well.

I called Alan. "I would like to talk to you about having your father test." "Why would you want to do that?" he asked. He sounded confused. I explained that in rare cases, siblings have been known not to share DNA and yet share the same parent. By testing his dad, we would know with absolute certainty one way or the other. Once I had finished my explanation, he agreed that his father should test. Alan also said he was not telling anyone else in the family about the test unless he proved to be my father. "Let me find out if my dad is agreeable to taking a test, and I'll call you back."

Within a half hour, Alan gave me the green light! He had spoken with his stepmother about the reason for the test, and she thought it was a good idea. As soon as Orval had taken the test, she would call to let me know. I ordered it from FTDNA, mainly because the results would be shown in centiMorgans. The numbers would tell me exactly how much DNA we shared. No matter the outcome, I could move on.

November 27, 2014

I just got off the phone with Orval McCullough's wife. She seemed quite nice and cordial. After she let me know that Orval had taken the test, she told me why she agreed to it. She was very interested in genealogy and had read that DNA testing was useful in expanding family trees. She felt I needed to know who my father was. I thanked her for agreeing and realized that in four to six weeks I would have an answer.

A NEW YEAR

JANUARY 12, 2015

I started the new year by taking inventory of what I knew for sure. My maternal DNA "Wall" was solidly in place. Margaret, Tom, Malcolm, Dave, Bruce, Cathy, Sue, and Carrie had all tested. And their results confirmed the birth certificate. That in itself proved the accuracy of DNA. I appreciated their willingness to help. And besides, they all wanted to know who my father was! Would 2015 be the year I'd find him?

JANUARY 21, 2015

Alan McCullough was on the phone. "Would you like to get together for a jam session?"

I replied, "Yeah, that would be great." Alan and I were now friends that shared a love of music. Two days later, he showed up at my door and the fun began. As we played through a number of pieces, I realized that our musical tastes were similar. Somewhere in the middle, we talked about the upcoming test results. I looked at Alan. What if he was my half-brother? We returned to the music. By the end of our session, Alan and I parted company closer than ever.

After Alan left, I assembled two plans. Plan one: Orval was my father. Alan and I would discuss how to approach the rest of his family. Plan two: Orval wasn't my father. I would continue my search and learn more about DNA testing. I needed to be prepared regardless of the outcome.

JANUARY 29, 2015

I assembled a "still looking for my father" plan. A key part was to seek out matches that defined my paternal side more effectively. Connie McKenzie reminded me that my father's line was indigenous to Scotland and Northern Ireland. That alone helped narrow things down. Connie said she would keep an eye out for test results that were a close match to mine.

FEBRUARY 1, 2015

Another month had arrived, and I still hadn't found a paternal match that showed real promise. The overlapping segments of DNA just weren't there. I reminded myself that it was a matter of time until I hit the jackpot. The longer it took, the more I reminded myself.

Another reality had set in. Only about twenty out of one hundred matches were responding to contact. That meant four-fifths of all my matches wouldn't be useful in my search. That was frustrating, especially when a relatively close match was involved. Not everybody testing was interested in genealogy. Three other reasons for testing were ethnic makeup, more distant haplogroup research, and health reports, through 23andMe. I wondered how many of the unresponsive matches held information crucial to my search.

FEBRUARY 13, 2015

Where were Orval's test results? They were taking longer than usual to arrive. I decided to check for new matches. There was nothing new on the first page. I was the administrator of Orval's kit. After opening his account, I looked at his home page as well. The waiting was over—his results *had been* posted. With just one look, I knew why he wasn't on my first page. I was nowhere to be found on his either. I had my answer. Zero. Zilch. Nada. No match. Orval definitely wasn't my father. I called Alan and told him the news. "That's too bad. I was hoping for a different outcome." "Me too." He and I would always remain friends, and make music from time to time. It wouldn't be quite the same, however.

Starting over *again*. I had been wrong once before. Make that twice. No brother. No father. I was numb emotionally. And the lesson learned? Never have anyone test solely on circumstantial evidence. I put plan B into action and returned to the tried and true.

The white pages were back in action. I searched for more individuals with different Irish and Scottish surnames. I used the letter scenario once again and mailed to Oregon residents that qualified. I kept moving forward. The emotional numbness worked to my advantage. I spent less time dwelling on not matching Orval than I did with Alan. I was back on the trail to find my father almost immediately.

FEBRUARY 19, 2015

Knowing the identity of my father would complete mine as well. That perspective was the driving force behind my persistent efforts. My "Wall" became the sorter for maternal or paternal matches. The paternal matches were used in triangulation to find a common ancestor. No matter how long it took, I would find him…

HOLD THE PRESSES!

FEBRUARY 26, 2015

Robert Liguori, my faithful DNA detective, had worked tirelessly for the last three months to solve my "Who's the daddy?" mystery. He was determined to find my father. Robert had consistently contacted other matches and asked for a list of family surnames in my behalf. He sent me pictures of potential fathers with Scottish surnames and similar physical character-istics to mine. He scoured my Ancestry matches looking for Scottish and Irish surnames that included extensive family trees. But until now, nothing convincing had surfaced.

It was 10:30 p.m. when I walked through the front door of our home. My choir had just finished a rehearsal and being wound up as usual, my normal activity was to check e-mails before doing anything else. On the way to get a glass of water in the kitchen, I approached the phone. The "new messages" light was blinking.

I was curious as to who called and hit the "play" button. The robot-like voice from the phone dutifully said, "You have four new messages." The first message was recorded at 7:00 p.m. The phone number had an out-of-state prefix. "Hi, this is Robert. I've found your father! Call me as soon as you get this message."

This was nothing new or unexpected. I was the frequent recipient of potential father information, including their pictures. I had sent Robert my senior yearbook picture to use as a visual reference when he looked at po-tential fathers. I was beginning to wonder if that had been a wise thing to do. Up until now, all evidence Robert sent led to a dead end. As much as I appreciated his enthusiasm and help, he reminded me of the little boy that cried "wolf."

I went on to message number two. Again, it was Robert repeating the first verbatim. The last two were repetitions of the first two. All of them were from Robert! Never had he been so adamant about claims in the past. I decided to call Robert in the morning—it was 1:30 a.m. on the east coast.

After listening to Robert's messages, I went to my PC and checked for new e-mails.

What? I had forty-three…all from Robert. Had he lost his mind? Now, I couldn't sleep. What information did they contain? Had he actually found my father? I was tempted to open them, but decided to wait until morning. I headed straight for bed!

I was up early, made breakfast, ate, pulled up the message center on my PC, grabbed the phone, and dialed Robert's number. I wondered what he'd found that was so urgent. Robert answered and quickly launched into his discovery. "Have you looked at your e-mails from me?" I replied "No, I wanted to do that while talking with you on the phone."

He said, "Open the first one, and tell me what you think." I said "Okay."

Before me were two photographs side by side. The one on the right was my high-school senior-yearbook picture I'd sent to Robert months ago. The picture on the left was new to me. The name under the picture was William McIntosh. I was looking at "my brother."

I was speechless. Robert waited a moment and then excitedly repeated his question. "What do you think?" "I think you are on to something" was all I could muster.

As I looked from one picture to the other, the similarities were very apparent. I saw my jaw, nose, head shape, ears, and eyebrows in William. He was born in 1853, ninety-eight years before me. How were we related? I was mesmerized by William's picture and forgot that Robert was waiting for me to say something. After a moment, he patiently said, "Open the next e-mail."

I was looking at information Robert compiled from my Ancestry account.

Using the process of triangulation, he had found four fourth cousin matches that matched each other. I was familiar with each, as they were located near the top on my first page of matches. They were in plain sight and I hadn't made the connection. Each had an extensive family tree. The surname in common was McIntosh. Robert found three generations of the McIntosh line that were identical in each tree. The common ancestor shared was Donald Gilbert. This meant that he was mine as well. Robert had found our common ancestor!

McIntosh? I looked at my Y test results. I had one McIntosh match that was never considered a contender. The genetic distance between us was too great to be genealogically relevant. This new evidence changed that. I dreamed of this day, but had no idea today would be it. The other e-mails added more information and pictures associated with the McIntosh discovery. I thanked Robert for his work. What an amazing find!

Next, I sent messages to each McIntosh match. The first was managed by John Lambertus, the son of the woman who had taken the test. Robert proactively contacted John and made arrangements for me to get in touch with him. John and I exchanged e-mails and decided to talk on the phone. Another first. I would be speaking with my first McIntosh relative. What would John be like?

I picked up the receiver and dialed his number. John answered, and his voice sounded warm and inviting. It turned out that John was a fountain of information. We started with the will of Donald Gilbert McIntosh and my three ancestors who fought in the Revolutionary War for the British! They were United Empire Loyalists better known as "Tories." I was fascinated and made every effort to soak it all up.

I asked if Robert shared any of my story with him. John told what he knew and I filled in the rest. I mentioned my involvement in music and asked if the McIntosh family had any musicians. John said, "Yes, there are many in the family." Before we ended our call, John gave me his mother's phone number. "Mom would love to talk with you, particularly because of your involvement in music." My conversation with John had been very positive. He seemed more like a first cousin, rather than a fourth cousin once removed.

LET THE MUSIC BEGIN

In the morning, I made a point of calling John's mom, Claire. As the conversation began, I could hear the excitement in her voice as we talked about the fact that DNA testing had led me to the McIntosh family. Claire wanted to hear my story from the beginning. When I had finished, Claire directed the conversation towards the topic of music.

She stated that the McIntosh family was teeming with musicians—instrumentalists, vocalists, voice teachers, opera singers. One in fact, had been lead trumpeter for Frank Sinatra in New York. I then explained that I was a voice coach and choir director. She was convinced that the McIntosh DNA was responsible for the musical talent that was so prevalent.

I was still reeling about the music when Claire asked a question. "Would you like a copy of *I Am McIntosh*? It's a booklet detailing the history of the McIntosh family. It starts with Gilbert McIntosh, born in 1700 in Scotland and follows his family line up until 1987." What? I couldn't believe my ears. I said yes in record time. She said it would have to be copied but would be glad to make one for me. I thanked Claire for offering a copy of this unexpected familial treasure. After the call ended, I was blown away by Claire's inclusive warmth and generosity.

The next day, I received a message on Ancestry from one of the other McIntosh fourth cousins. Her name was Barbara. I had sent a copy of my story in the first message to her. I opened hers and began reading. "Don, I am so delighted that you have found out so much!" She went on to share information about her part of the family, including all the musical talent they possessed. She finished with, "I have a written history done by some cousins called *I Am MacKintosh*."‡ I would happy to make a copy and send it to you."

As soon as I was done with reading, I responded immediately with "Yes Barbara, I would love a copy of *I Am MacKintosh*. Soon after that message left my PC, another message from Barbara appeared. "Great. I will overnight it to you." In a split second, I gave her my address, and the next day FedEx delivered!

A day later, I was on the phone with Claire to let her know that I had received a copy of *I Am MacKintosh*. She was happy, as it was going to take longer than she expected to reproduce it. Amazing! I received two offers to send *"I Am MacKintosh"* and had a copy in my hands in twenty-four hours. I was astounded by the generosity of both Claire and Barbara. Their desire to include me in the McIntosh family seemed very much like the reception I received from the Blackstones, starting with my first meeting with Margaret.

---

‡ The surname McIntosh is a variation of MacKintosh or Macintosh.

I got on my PC to send Barbara an e-mail, thanking her for the *"MacKintosh"* book. As soon as that was sent, a number of messages from Robert appeared. They must have come in while I was writing to Barbara. Okay, what could he possibly have sent? Maybe he had additional information about the McIntosh family.

I opened the first message and couldn't believe what I saw. Robert said he had found another three fourth cousin matches on Ancestry with the same scenario as the McIntosh matches. Each matched each other and me, the same surname was in each of their family trees and none matched my maternal side. This time, however, the surname was Murray. I was blown away by Robert's successful sleuthing. How did he do it?

I got on the phone and called him. We talked about his find. He was as thrilled as I was. He asked if I had looked at all the other messages, to which I replied "no." He said as usual, "Open them and take a look." I looked at each message. Robert had followed the trees of both families toward the present and had made a flow chart that was easy to read. The names and dates were all there. With the last e-mail, a big chunk of the puzzle was put into place.

Robert found that a marriage had taken place in 1925 between Keith McIntosh and Margaret Murray in Canada and included the documentation to prove it. So that was why I had the two sets of triangulation on Ancestry! A McIntosh had married a Murray. After I had finished my conversation with Robert, a simple, yet satisfying thought crossed my mind. I was getting closer.

MARCH 1, 2015

Things had moved at a dizzying pace. I used *I Am MacKintosh* book in my search for more information. Every surname that was connected to the family was listed in alphabetical order at the end of the book. I quickly found Donald Gilbert McIntosh and turned to the page that I needed to read. Following his descendants trail, I reached Keith McIntosh, Donald's great grandson. There was an entire page devoted to Keith and his family.

After Keith and Margaret were married, Keith, his father Peter and brother Bert built and operated two creameries in Saskatchewan, Canada. In 1937, both creameries were sold and the families moved to Corvallis, Oregon. There they purchased the Green Valley Creamery. Accompanying Keith and Margaret were their two children, Jeanne and Stuart. Moved to Corvallis? Nancy was from Corvallis. This was looking very promising. Could I have found my family?

Robert, who was always ahead of the game, was pretty convinced that Stuart was my father. He had supplied me with my first picture of Stuart. The 1947 Corvallis high-school yearbook showed Stuart standing with members of the snow skiing club in front of the school. His image was small, making it difficult to clearly see facial features. I didn't care. I was just happy to have it.

So, he was on the ski team. I had never snow skied a day in my life. Now, I had my first tidbit of information on something he liked to do. Wait a minute…How was Robert able to find that? Somehow, he had accessed the picture on the Internet.

THE PHONE CALL

In his next e-mail, Robert had found Stuart's obituary from the Roseburg, Oregon, newspaper. His full name was James Howard Stuart McIntosh, with the nickname "Stu" inserted. He had passed away in 2008 and was buried at the National Military Cemetery in Roseburg. After reading that much of his obituary, I paused for a moment.

If Stuart proved to be my father, I realized we would never have the opportunity to meet during this life. In the past, I had glossed over the possibility of my birth father being deceased, without dwelling on it. Now, I needed to give this scenario a more prominent position in my thinking. I had no idea as to how this would affect me emotionally.

I continued reading through the 2008 obituary in search of surviving family members and wrote down the names listed. It mentioned that he married Delores Pumala in 1955, ending in divorce, with no children. In 1973, he married Bette, who had two children from her previous marriage. His sister, Jeanne, was not mentioned anywhere. Bette had passed in 2010, and his niece, Jan, in 2014. His nephew, Keith Liggett, was living in Canada at the time. He would be my closest connection to Stuart and the only one that could confirm him as my father. Three questions loomed in front of me. Was Keith still alive, and would he be willing to test and how would I locate him?

Diana was on top of my dilemma and did some detective work to help me out. She found Keith's contact information online. She handed me a sticky note with his phone number written on it. Only forty-eight hours after Robert had sent Stuart's obituary, I had the phone in hand and cold-called Keith. I was an experienced cold-caller from a job I'd had years ago. But the reason for this cold-call was entirely different. What I said would determine Keith's response. I felt much the same as when I approached Margaret's door for the first time.

There were glaring differences, however. With Margaret, the family knew of my existence. I had official documentation and six months to prepare for contact. And in Keith's case, the McIntosh family knew nothing and there were no records to substantiate anything. In forty-eight hours, I had gone from no knowledge of Keith to calling him about taking a DNA test to confirm Stuart as my father. What would Keith's reaction be? Would he even answer the phone? The fear of rejection was quickly eclipsed by my desire to know if Stuart was my birth father.

I dialed his number with butterflies in my stomach. Three times it rang, and a male voice answered. I asked if Keith was there, to which he answered,

"I'm Keith." After introducing myself, I began by explaining that I had been working on genealogy and family history. I had made the discovery two days earlier that we were quite possibly related. I thought I had said that in a calm, convincing manner. He responded by saying, "I'm a bit skeptical about this." I told him I was too, being that all the information was forty-eight hours old and I was still processing everything myself.

Keith continued, "Could you tell me how we might be related?" Okay, I could share a bit more of my story. I hadn't wanted to go into the adoption part just yet. I responded by telling him that I lived in Oregon and then asked if his grandparents names were Keith and Margaret McIntosh. He said they were. I was positive that the right person was on the line. I continued by saying that because they had lived in Oregon, and I had been born and raised there, we could possibly be cousins.

At that point, I felt confident in asking Keith if he would take a DNA test in my next sentence. Diana was standing nearby, listening to my side of the conversation. It had to have been frustrating not being able to hear everything that was said.

Then the granddaddy of curve balls was hurled my direction with Keith's next question. "Exactly how are we cousins?" What? I was between a rock and a hard place. I blurted out the first thing that came to my mind. "Give me a moment to get the paperwork," trying to buy some time. With the receiver pressed tightly against my chest, I quietly repeated to Diana what Keith had said, and asked, "What should I tell him?"

Diana responded wisely. "Tell him the whole story." Yikes, the whole story? That meant talking about my adoption. How would he react to that? Diana was right, and I told her so. Returning to my conversation with Keith, I asked him if he wanted the whole story. His reply was simply, "Yes, the whole story."

This was it. I proceeded to share the entire tale, beginning with my adoption, followed by finding my birth mother, and concluding with my last sentence: "Based on the DNA, genealogical and circumstantial evidence, I believe that your uncle, Stuart McIntosh, is my father and you are my first cousin." Done. What would be his reply? Would he hang up the phone? Would he be in shock?

After a second of silence, Keith's response came. "That's really interesting!" That was not the response I had expected. He followed that by asking me to e-mail everything that pertained to my research—the genealogy, DNA test results, triangulation information, and pictures of William, Stuart, Nancy, and myself. I quickly said, "Absolutely." Next I notched up my courage and asked, "Would you be willing to take a DNA test to help confirm Stuart as my father?"

He said he would look over the materials I was sending and get back with an answer in a few days. After thanking him for talking to me, I realized his response was definitely better than "no." Once the conversation ended, I quickly assembled the requested materials, along with my positive thoughts and e-mailed them to Keith. I gave it my best shot. If he decided to test, would Keith share enough DNA with me to be my first cousin?

THE AFTERSHOCK

MARCH 4, 2015
Today, an e-mail from my possible Canadian cousin, Keith, arrived. I waited a moment before opening it. Had he decided that my information and pictures were credible, and more importantly, was he going to test?

"It was a bit of a shock. I was always the son that Stu and Delores couldn't have" were the first words written. It sounded like he was taken back by what

I had told him over the phone. I got it! Stuart never had any children biologically. In the obituary, nothing was mentioned about any offspring. And by what Keith said, he and Stuart must have had a close and loving relationship.

After sharing some McIntosh family history, I went back to review the paragraph that included a subject near and dear to my heart. The first sentence began "Yes, the music is interesting. Mom was first chair cello at OSU and Stanford." His parents met at Stanford and started a family in Palo Alto, California. The family had made numerous trips to Corvallis each year. From there, he was back to the subject of music.

"There was always music in the house. We never had less than two pianos. Often more. The cello, clarinets, guitar, flute, and so on. Both mom and dad had great voices and were soloists in various musical productions. Church choirs, light opera and so on." As music had played a major role in my life, I was thrilled to hear about the musical talents of his mother, Jeanne and how music had played a significant role in their home.

Many times in my life, people had asked where my musical talents had come from and I always said, "I had no idea." Now I knew. The music had come from both my maternal and paternal lines! Never again would I have a problem telling anyone where my musical talents came from. Along with music, I had begun to see how DNA passed down talents, mannerisms, gestures, and physical similarities.

Then Keith shared information about himself. He was primarily a writer and also taught snow skiing. Included was a resume of his journalistic background. It all made sense. When Keith and I had spoken the first time, I was amazed that he had wanted the whole story. Any journalist worth their salt would have asked for the same thing.

Then, suddenly in the next sentence, he wrote, "I have no problem with the DNA deal." Keith had decided to test! The information I sent to him must have tipped the scales in favor of testing. If someone called me out of the blue and said they were related to me, I would have probably wanted proof, just as Keith had. I must have earned his trust.

I immediately responded by thanking him for agreeing to test, sharing information about his family and his relationship with Stuart. I couldn't get over it—he had agreed to test! I was relieved. I took a risk and ordered an FTDNA test kit a day before our phone call. It paid off. Now I wouldn't have to send it back, or try to find someone else to sell it to. I was just being prepared.

It took between five and ten weeks for the results to post once the testing company had received the test. I took advantage of that time by looking for any other possible McIntosh–Murray unions in all my new information. As I began that project, something occurred to me. What if my father had been adopted as well? This question had been staring at me from the beginning of my father search, and I hadn't realized it.

Adoptee

That was a word I had lived with my whole life. In the genetic genealogy (the combination of genealogy and DNA) world, the word "adoptee" was represented by different words: nonpaternal (or paternity) event. I was an *NPE*§. What about my father? No, he couldn't have been. DNA was telling me as much.

I had learned my lesson from the McCullough experience a year earlier. I was checking into every aspect possible. I wanted to avoid another dead end.

---

§ NPE (nonpaternal event) is a term used in genetic genealogy to describe any event that has caused a break in the link between an hereditary surname from that of the biological father. The definition excludes minor changes in the spelling of the surname and is implicitly limited to events after the relevant branch of the surname became hereditary (Courtesy: ISOGG wiki).

LOOKING FOR STANLEYS

MARCH 6, 2015

The DNA matches kept coming in! I was contacted by Jack Stanley, a predicted third cousin match from 23andMe. "Do you happen to have any Stanleys in your family tree?"

I told him, "I'll check and get back to you." I searched my new genealogical information and found an Adeline Stanley. She was Stuart's maternal grandmother. I e-mailed Jack this information. He said he would see if there was a connection. We were predicted to be third cousins, after all. It would be amazing if Adeline was the key to a common ancestor.

I quickly received a reply from Jack. "Adeline Stanley is my great grandfather's sister." We shared great-great-grandparents as common ancestors. Jack and I were third cousins! DNA confirmed what genealogy suggested. Once again, genetic genealogy had worked its magic.

PICTURES, DOCUMENTS, AND AUTOGRAPHS, OH MY!

MARCH 7, 2015

Claire's son, John Lambertus, sent documentation consisting of a will and land grants that belonged to the McIntosh family. Three generations were mentioned, including the name of my great-great-grandfather, Archibald Wilberforce McIntosh. This was invaluable from a genealogical standpoint. John had really come through for me!

I was proficient at finding public family trees on Ancestry. I chalked up two more for both McIntosh and Murray. I couldn't believe the amount of new information in my possession. As the evidence grew, so did my list of new relatives.

MARCH 17, 2015

I knew my way to the Benton County Museum and could have driven there blindfolded. I called Mary Gallagher and set up a time and date to do more research. The best part was I had the surname of McIntosh to work with. She was excited to hear the news and would do some research before I arrived.

Two seconds after hanging up, the phone rang. It was Carrie, Margaret's granddaughter, who lived in Corvallis. Her timing was impeccable. She said enthusiastically, "I have something to share that you'll be excited to see. I found grandma's yearbooks!" Now I was excited as well. I told her I would be at the museum to research the McIntosh line. "Would it be alright if I stopped by after I'm finished?" She said with emphasis, "Yes, that's fine. When you get here, I want you to go to the kitchen table, sit down and look at what I've found. No talking, just look." As hard as that might have been for me, I said, "No problem!"

After the call, my mind went back to a conversation my cousin, Dave Robnett, which I had two weeks earlier. We discussed the whereabouts of Margaret's high-school yearbooks. He thought they were in his basement, but wasn't sure where. I updated him on my search and why the yearbooks were so important to locate. He said he was out of town, but Carrie was house-sitting for them. Maybe she would help.

I called Carrie and asked if she wouldn't mind looking for the yearbooks. She agreed to do some sleuthing in Dave's basement for me. From the beginning of my search, Carrie had been one of my most ardent supporters, ready to help at a moment's notice. This was her chance. She was definitely the best person for this job!

Two days later, at 10:00 a.m., I arrived at the museum ready to see what Mary had dug up. She met me in the library and with a smile, pointed to a stack of books and papers on the table. My jaw really hurt as it hit the floor. Exceeding my expectations would've been an understatement. It reminded me of an episode of the PBS television show *Finding Your Roots*. The documentation was conveniently laid out, ready for me to look at. Knowing the surname made all the difference!

"I have some other things to take care of. If you need anything, I'll be back in a little while to help." After thanking her, I realized no one else was in the room. The quiet helped me focus. I started at the top of the stack. There were two obituaries from the Corvallis newspaper.

One was of my possible great-grandfather, Peter Howard McIntosh, and the other was his other son, Donald "Bert" McIntosh. Next was a full-page advertisement on the back of the 1950 Corvallis phone directory. Featured was the Green Valley Creamery, owned and operated by the McIntosh brothers.

Inside the directory, under the letter "M" were the residential addresses and phone numbers of the three McIntosh families. At the bottom of the stack, Mary had saved the best for last. The 1947 Corvallis High School yearbook. I was looking at James Howard Stuart McIntosh's senior picture. My full attention focused on the image before me. His nose, jaw line, eyes, ears, and mouth all were similar to mine.

While I looked at Stuart's picture, the night of February 26 flashed in my mind. Robert's phone messages and e-mails, the picture of William, and the four fourth cousin matches all stood out vividly. The flood of new DNA, genealogical, and circumstantial evidence had strengthened Stuart's likelihood of being my father. It was mind-boggling just to contemplate. Mary returned to the library. "You can make copies of everything you've looked at." "Thanks, I will." Before leaving the museum, I thanked Mary for everything she had done since my first visit. I got in the car and headed for Carrie's. It seemed to take forever to get to her home. What exactly had she found?

As I walked toward her door, Carrie was waiting there to welcome me. She reminded me to sit at the kitchen table, open the top yearbook that she had marked with several sticky notes, and to do no talking. One of the notes was larger, patterned, and colored differently than the others. "Open to that one first," she said. Her excitement was almost at the level of mine. When I opened to that page, I was speechless. Tears began to form.

It was J. H. Stuart McIntosh, along with other members of the student body council. He was vice president as a junior. The stunning part was he had signed his picture. He knew Margaret! It was my first look at his handwriting—"Stu McIntosh." How did he and Margaret know each other? Did they have a class together? I wasn't talking. I was still speechless.

The other pages Carrie had marked held the answers. The next sticky note was attached to the school orchestra. Margaret played cello throughout her high-school career. I opened to that page and found her in the cello section in the back row. Margaret was the last one on the right. As I continued to scan the picture, on the front row, second from the end on the right, was "McIntosh"! Stuart played the violin. The next marked page featured the school yearbook staff. There was Margaret, in the back row. And Stuart? In the front. I turned to the 1945 yearbook. The marked page once again showed Margaret and Stuart in the orchestra.

Something unexpected had been found in the last yearbook from 1944. Another picture of the orchestra had been tagged. Margaret was standing on the right end of the front row. In the middle of that same row, holding a cello, was another McIntosh—Stuart's older sister, Jeanne! My maternal and possible paternal aunts in the same picture, in the same row, holding the same type of instrument. There weren't words to describe this. What crossed my mind next hit like a ton of bricks. I had inherited my love for music from both sides of the family.

Stuart, Jeanne, and Margaret shared activities where students interacted more than usual with each other. Both music and being on the yearbook staff were considered extracurricular activities. Music, like sports, create a bond between students, both socially and emotionally. And concerts, like games, became some of the most memorable moments during high school for young musicians.

In small towns, school music concerts were well attended by families of those participating. Because of that, it seemed quite likely that the Blackstone and McIntosh families met on more than one occasion. It stood to reason that Nancy and Stuart met during those events.

Before I left Carrie's for home, she shared her experience associated with finding her grandmother's yearbooks. "You were trying to locate grandma's high-school yearbooks to see if there might be a photo, or any other information regarding your father. You asked my uncle who was out of town at the time, if he might know where they were. Uncle David said that he thought that they were somewhere in his basement. Since my aunt and uncle where out of town, you asked me to look for them. I knew of several boxes filled with older papers and books brought from my grandmother's home and slowly went through them, piece by piece. After several minutes and not having any luck, I decided to start heading upstairs. But then something told me that I should turn around to look for them. And there they were, right behind me, on top of a stack of boxes. It was almost like they were set out, waiting for me to find. After returning home, I called you right away to tell you the good news. I decided to peruse them first before you came down. To my surprise, I found several items that I knew would make you very happy. I flagged them, ready for your visit. That's why I suggested that you sit down before opening the yearbooks."

By the time she finished, my speech had returned. "Carrie, words can't accurately describe how I feel. You'll never know how much it means to me. Thank you." After I left, my thoughts went back to those yearbooks and the experience that had just happened. I savored it for the next ninety minutes as I made my way back to Portland.

After arriving home, I called Carrie and thanked her once again. She gently reminded me of a prediction she'd made when I began my search. "I told you that he would be right under our noses if we knew just where to look." I was beginning to believe Carrie was right!

The Y for testing

March 23, 2015

Claire, my McIntosh fourth cousin, was the target of a phone call I made the next day. I had to catch her up on the newest revelations, especially yesterday in Corvallis. She was thrilled with what she heard. Then I asked her about the role music had played in the family. The *I Am McIntosh* book listed several family members with musical backgrounds. I wanted to get Claire's personal insight. She eagerly proceeded to share some of the family's musical history. One of her cousins in particular had been first chair trumpet for Frank Sinatra when he performed in New York City!

Toward the end of our call, Claire said something very unexpected. "I have a first cousin Gary McIntosh, who lives in the Portland area, and he is taking a Y 111 test. John and I talked him into doing it." "Oh my gosh, Claire. You've given me the greatest gift. I was hoping to find someone to take that test and you've supplied me with exactly what I've needed." Connie had been adamant about a Y test confirming my surname. Gary's results would answer the McIntosh question once and for all.

TWISTS, TURNS, AND TREES

MARCH 27, 2015
Keith's Family Finder test was mailed out a week ago. He received it yesterday, took the test, and mailed it back to me today. Once in my possession, I would send it on its way to Houston. In about six to eight weeks, I would know if Stuart was my father. Simple. I shifted into the waiting mode, something I was very familiar with.

MARCH 28, 2015
Each day, I regularly checked for new matches at all three companies. This morning, I started with Ancestry. Three close matches had appeared. All were in the third to fourth cousin range. The administrator for each was Wilma Hoover. This indicated that they were very likely related to each other, but how? Out of my top fifteen matches only these three were unknowns. But where did they fit into my tree? Maternal or paternal?

I stayed on my Ancestry page as I called Carrie. Both Tom and she had tested there. "Carrie, I have three new close matches on Ancestry. Could you look to see if you match any of them?" I gave her the information on each. After a moment, she said, "I don't match any of them." I thanked her. One down and one remaining. I had Tom's information, so I logged into his account. I checked his matches page, and none matched him either. So who did they match? A very small family tree was connected to one. None of the surnames sounded familiar. I had gone as far as I could without help.

I messaged Wilma Hoover and asked about any surnames that hadn't been included on the tree. I explained to her, "I am adopted, and looking for my birth father. I have figured out that we must be related through my paternal side. I have also taken the Y-test. The results have given me a number of surnames, but I don't know which is my father's. If you could send me a list of surnames you have, I could compare it to mine. My hope is to find my birth father and his family. Any information you could provide would be appreciated!"

She messaged back, wanting to help, but was computer challenged. I asked her if we could talk over the phone to which she said okay. At the bottom, she added, "I have not found any new names."

I didn't waste any time in calling. "Is Wilma there?" "That's me!" I heard a sense of humor mixed in with the sound of her voice. I went into a bit more detail as I spoke, ending with, "I was wondering if you could tell me the surnames in your family tree."

"Honey, I'm eighty-seven years old. Can I mail you a copy of my family surnames?"

She had made an offer I couldn't refuse. "Absolutely." She asked for my address and said she'd get right on it. When it arrived three days later, I studied the list of surnames. Not one matched any on my list. This mystified and frustrated me at the same time. What was the connection between us? I called Wilma to let her know how much I appreciated the work she'd done. I also had to tell her there were no surname matches. She sounded as disappointed as I was. I thanked her and moved on to other leads.

APRIL 1, 2015

It was time to call Gary McIntosh. Claire had given me his phone number during one of our calls. He had taken the Y 111 test and lived in the Portland area. Earlier, I had come across Gary in my "McIntosh" book. If Stuart was my father, he would be my fourth cousin. An almost exact match would have to occur to prove that McIntosh was my surname. "Hi. Is Gary there?" I asked. "I'm Gary." His voice was upbeat and sounded like a tenor. His energy level seemed to match mine. As we talked, the connection between us grew. Gary sounded excited about the possibility of having another cousin and was glad he could take the test to help out. We decided to get together after the results were in. I was looking forward to meeting Gary in person. If we did match, he would be my first physical encounter with a paternal relative. I was more anxious than ever to see the results of his test.

APRIL 3, 2015

A summary of Stuart's military service was now in my possession. He served in the army from August 1948 until he was honorably discharged on August 1, 1950. Thirteen months of that was served in Korea, finally returning home to Corvallis approximately two weeks before conception occurred. I was going to send for a formal copy of his records from the National Military Personnel Records, located in St. Louis, Missouri.

APRIL 5, 2015

Two setbacks happened today. We had both served in the army. I wanted to compare our service records. I looked through the information provided by the government related to accessing military records. To my disappointment, only the legal next of kin were able to receive a copy. Since Stuart wasn't legally my father, I was out of luck. Later, I was notified by the US post office that there was a problem with the package from Keith in Canada. It wasn't deliverable as addressed. The package had to be sent back to Canada, and any corrections needed to be made by the sender. I wondered how long that was going to take.

Something very positive entered my thoughts. For the first time in my life, I realized that if the surname McIntosh was proven to be mine, I would finally have one to live honorably for. That hadn't occurred to me as an Anderson. My adoptive parents never mentioned honoring the family name. I wondered how many other adoptees had this experience.

Tomorrow was my birthday. Normally in the past when my family asked what I wanted as a gift, I was hard-pressed to come up with an answer. This year was different. I knew the answer...to find my father.

For the last couple of days, I had been searching Ancestry's "public trees" section. I used the name of Donald Gilbert McIntosh to find how many trees he was listed in. I compared the owner's names of the public trees to the list of surnames in the "McIntosh" book. So far, I had found thirty and would keep looking for more. One tree in particular caught my eye. The owner was the wife of a potential McIntosh second cousin. Included was the direct line of McIntoshes who had moved from Canada to Corvallis in 1937. One crucial piece of documentation was the 1925 Canadian marriage record for Stuart's parents, Keith McIntosh and Margaret Murray. This public tree contained the most genealogical information I'd found regarding Stuart's family. I decided to message the owner tomorrow. What a find!

After my experience contacting Keith, this would be a piece of cake. I had revealed to Keith that his uncle fathered a child he wasn't aware of. It had been a bit of a shock. Second cousins were distant enough from the situation to lessen the trauma that commonly surrounds an illegitimate birth in a family. Tomorrow, I would find out if that was the case.

The next morning I messaged the owner of the tree. I briefly explained the reason for contacting her. Because of all the details I wanted to share, I asked if it would be alright for me to phone her. She said that would be fine, and she ended the message by including her phone number and a good time for me to call. I thanked her and made plans to call in a few days. I was sure she could shed some light on Stuart as well.

APRIL 26, 2015

Wow, I just got off the phone with the possible second cousin's wife. We had a great conversation! She asked for more detail about my story, specifically regarding Stuart and Nancy. She then told about her husband's family, the Green Valley Creamery and their connection to Corvallis. Her husband's father was a first cousin to Stuart and about six years older. Next, I wanted to get down to business and talk about DNA testing for her husband. I gave it my best shot. "I was hoping that your husband would be willing to take a DNA test in order to prove that Stuart is my father." She said, "The decision to test would be up to him. I will talk to him about it." She thought that DNA testing was a good thing. It's too bad she wasn't the one taking the test. I told her I understood and that a letter would be sent to him with information about testing. I thanked her for speaking with me. She seemed like a nice person who understood my predicament. The call had definitely been worth my time.

Later, an e-mail from Robert contained the obituary of the second cousin's father. I was amazed by the timing. First, the phone call, then the obituary. The second cousin and three other siblings were listed as surviving family members. Diana went to work and found contact information on the Internet. I composed a letter and explained the reason for contacting them.

I mailed the letters the next morning. Would these cousins be willing to test? I remembered some sage council I received from an acquaintance at the DNA conference in Houston regarding the decision whether or not to ask someone to test. "Remember, if you don't ask, the answer will always be 'no.'" I had followed that advice more than once.

APRIL 27, 2015
This morning, an e-mail arrived from the last of the four original McIntosh matches.

The sender was Barbara Sanchez. As with the other three, I had sent an introduction and my story. Her message contained words of welcome, followed by an excited response to what I had written. Barbara wanted to know how we were related. I started by sharing what I knew and asked if she was aware of the "McIntosh" book. To my amazement, she told me her father was one of the authors!

I told her Archibald Wilberforce McIntosh was our common ancestor. I descended from his first wife Christina and Barbara from his second wife Elsie. She was a generation closer to Archibald and technically my half second cousin, once removed. She ended with something startling. It had been ten years since her last contact with a McIntosh family member. Barbara thanked me for reaching out to her. Since I had given her my phone number in my e-mail, she shared hers as well. Barbara's correspondence felt like something a close first cousin would have sent.

After Barbara's e-mail, I decided a prewritten copy of "My Story" should be available to send when requested. That would save me from having to compose a new version each time I was asked to share it. As my story grew, I would add to it as needed.

APRIL 28, 2015

Our phone rang. I looked at the caller I.D. It was Barbara Sanchez. We had a great conversation and I learned more about her parents. Once again, she thanked me for reestablishing contact with the family. After more details about my journey, she said convincingly, "You are a McIntosh…" I couldn't help but ask, "How do you know that?"

"I just know." Those three words made an indelible impression on me. Before saying good-bye, she shared one final observation. "I just feel a connection with you." I was beginning to wonder if the McIntosh family carried a psychic gene in their DNA.

DEAR MR. ANDERSON…

APRIL 29, 2015

An e-mail arrived from one of the possible McIntosh second cousins. It began with "Dear Mr. Anderson." That sounded formal and distant. His opening set the tone. "I received your letter…" he continued by stating that the contents of the letter were sketchy. He wanted to know exactly who I was, and why I thought I was a McIntosh before he would share any information.

His need to be cautious was understandable. I felt frustrated at this point. Much of my frustration was due to the status of Keith's test. Taking a moment, I gathered my thoughts on how to answer. The evidence to prove my claim was legitimate. Transparency could make the difference as to whether or not information was shared in return.

I spent the next two hours assembling everything and sent him the works. Included in the e-mail were my story, my McIntosh family tree on Ancestry.

com, DNA research I had collected on my matches, proof established through triangulation, pictures of Nancy, Stuart, William McIntosh, and myself. I also included a list of references to contact regarding my character. I felt like I had crafted a resume for a potential employer.

By the time I finished and sent the e-mail, my initial frustration had disappeared.

I then realized he had no prior knowledge of me, or what my intentions might be. Given the circumstances, I probably would have reacted similarly. I had learned how to prepare a set of e-mail attachments to have ready for other family members who might want similar proof.

APRIL 30, 2015

Today, I reflected on my frustration from the day before. When my possible second cousin responded to my letter by asking for more information about me and the research I had done, I wasn't exactly thrilled about the unexpected request. Now, I was glad I had done it. But had I included everything needed to convince them to test? Had I said or included anything that might cause them to ultimately say no?

MAY 1, 2015

I received a response from the second cousin. The beginning of his e-mail was less formal and a bit friendlier. He said he was impressed with my research. He thanked me for all the information and said he would share it with his brother. I was glad the information I sent tipped the scales in my favor.

Later in the day, an e-mail from the other brother showed up. He said, after reading through all the documentation sent to him by his brother, that I had done an impressive job of connecting myself to the McIntosh family tree. He proposed a teleconference call between the three of us to discuss testing in more detail. Three different dates and times were listed to choose from. I chose the next day at 2:00 p.m. After a couple of e-mail exchanges, the call was set. The idea of a three-way call intrigued me. I would be speaking to both of them tomorrow. My reoccurring thought was again…would they decide to test?

May 2, 2015

The phone rang exactly at two o'clock. I had been trying to anticipate questions and/or concerns they might express. I believed I was ready to speak to them. I picked up the receiver. After introductions had been made, I explained what was involved when taking a DNA test. I also made it known that I would cover the cost of the tests. I was able to answer all their questions in a satisfactory manner, except for one. They had concerns regarding their privacy.

I never gave much thought to privacy issues associated with DNA testing. As an adoptee it wasn't a concern, mainly because of the openness needed to get answers I was looking for. But to them privacy was a real concern. I said I wasn't familiar with the privacy policies that existed and would inquire into steps taken by the testing companies to protect the privacy of those who tested and get back to them. Their decision to test now rested on the answer I provided. This wrinkle surprised me, having never encountered it before. I needed to educate myself as quickly as possible.

May 4, 2015

This morning I e-mailed Emily Aulicino, one of the local Oregon DNA experts. I posed the privacy issues in the form of a question. As usual, she provided good information. Anyone taking a DNA test must sign the release form. If they didn't want to sign their real name, a false one would work just as well, assuring anonymity. Later I spoke with FTDNA, and they confirmed what Emily had said. It was against company policy to post results without a signature. The bottom line was if test results couldn't be posted, the reason for testing vanished.

MAY 16, 2015

I had the answer and sent it on to my second cousins. One messaged back saying I would be notified of their decision in the next few days. There was nothing more to be done. I reviewed the gravity of my situation. From December 2013, every spare moment had been dedicated to finding my birth father. I had spent countless hours learning about DNA testing, contacting matches, and building a mentor network. It all came down to four DNA tests. One to confirm McIntosh as my surname. The other three would answer whether or not Stuart was my father.

For the next two days, I compared my search for Nancy to my current one. Using an official document was very different when compared to DNA testing. In six months, I ended up at Margaret's door and ten minutes later, I spoke with Nancy. By comparison, the search for my father started with two pieces of faulty nonidentifying information. In eighteen months, I took nine DNA tests, uncovered my Celtic roots, triangulated matches on Ancestry, searched family trees, learned to interpret test results, and reached out to newfound cousins. With those four remaining tests, would I finally see light at the end of the tunnel?

MAY 19, 2015

Two pieces of good news. Number one—the second cousins had decided to test. Hallelujah! Apparently, the information sent to them satisfied their privacy concerns. They told me that they would sign the release forms.

Number two—both Claire and Barbara took the Family Finder tests. Their results had posted, making it official. The centiMorgans had proven Claire to be my fourth cousin and Barbara my second cousin once removed.

That's what the tests results said. But because of the bonds that had begun to form with each, they really were family.

MAY 20, 2015

With Keith's test missing in action, I ordered a replacement one week ago. The post office could no longer track the package, as it continued to float between California and Canada. After I spoke to USPS employees, it was decided that the label had been removed, which discontinued further efforts to pinpoint where the package was. The new kit arrived today and was sent to Keith before I went to my DNA class. I e-mailed him about the replacement test that was headed his direction.

MAY 21, 2015

I had a nice talk with Claire today. She continued to paint a picture of the McIntosh family that transcends the information in my "McIntosh Book." Her perspective was giving me a personal peek into the lives of family members I wouldn't get any other way. Once again, my growing relationship with Claire feels much closer than that of a fourth cousin that genealogy suggests.

MAY 22, 2015

FTDNA informed me that one of my second cousin's tests had arrived in Houston. The other shouldn't be far behind.

OF ROYAL BLOOD

MAY 25, 2015

Jack Stanley, my third cousin match through 23andMe, notified me that I was related to Robert the Bruce, King of Scotland (b. 1274 and d. 1329). He set up an account for me on geni.com, where an extensive pedigree chart had been established detailing the lineage of the Bruce family. Second, Jack had completed the research needed and made a successful connection between the Stanley and Bruce lines. This was exciting. My great-grandmother, Addie Stanley had been my key connection to royalty. And after doing the math, I claimed Robert the Bruce as my twentieth great-grandfather.

COMINGS AND GOINGS

MAY 27, 2015
FTDNA had just confirmed the receipt of the other second cousin's test and estimated that both tests results would be available to view between June 17 and July 1. That was good to hear. I still hadn't heard anything regarding the status of the Canadian test. Where in the heck could it be?

The next day, Keith's new test kit showed up in my mailbox. I had just enough time to mail it to a location in Montana that he used as an alternative for sending and receiving packages. I made a beeline for my DNA class right after that task was accomplished. After class, I sent Keith an e-mail as a heads-up about the new arrival.

JUNE 3, 2015
Guess what showed up in Canada today? The first test package sent by Keith! He decided to take a picture of it and then e-mailed me the proof of its return. Only one needed to be sent back to FTDNA in Houston. I was worried that the first test might have been tampered with or damaged in transit. Because of that, I advised Keith to take the new test at its arrival point in Montana, mail it directly to Houston, and then mail the old one to me. He would let me know when he had done just that. I was relieved to hear the news.

'TIS THE SURNAME

JUNE 4, 2015

Gary McIntosh and his sister Patty both e-mailed me this morning. Gary wanted me to know that he and his family would be spectators of the Grand Floral Parade at the Memorial Coliseum in Portland two days from now. He shared his phone number in case I had a free moment to call. In an earlier e-mail, I had mentioned my involvement with the festival, specifically during parade time at the coliseum. Gary also made a point of wanting to meet in person if I had a moment. It would be my first physical contact with a McIntosh!

His sister Patti had heard about me from Gary. She wanted to introduce herself and find out when would be a good time to talk on the phone. To my surprise, she was living in the Corvallis area. I couldn't wait to tell her where my birth parents were both from. Later, I e-mailed both Gary and Patty pictures of William McIntosh and myself. William was their great-grandfather, and I was his "brother." Both sent quick responses back, and both remarked how striking the resemblances were. In my last message to Gary that day, I told him he would hear from me around 9:30 the next morning.

JUNE 6, 2015

It was Parade Day, and at 9:30 a.m., I dialed Gary's number. I had spoken to him on the phone before, but this time we would meet. "Hi, we are in Section S," he said enthusiastically. I surveyed that direction. I had no idea what Gary looked like or where he and his family were seated. So I asked, "Could you wave at me?" Immediately, I saw a man out in an aisle wildly waving his arms. That could only be Gary. He was about fifty yards away from my position on the floor, standing next to the fifteenth row. My heart was pounding as I quickly made my way to his location. When I approached, he extended his arms and with at least five hundred people watching, exuberantly exclaimed, "Hello cousin! Give me a hug!"

I hugged him. The five hundred spectators surrounding us must have wondered what was going on. I couldn't have cared less. Gary's demonstrative expression was amazing for two reasons. First, he had welcomed me as family without knowing the Y test results. And I wasn't used to that kind of demonstrative inclusion by a relative. "How do you know that I'm a McIntosh?" I asked. His answer: "I can just tell." Ah, the McIntosh ESP gene was working once again. After the hug, Gary introduced me to his wife, daughter and her family. They were warm and friendly as well.

If that wasn't enough, when I returned home after the parade, I checked e-mails on my PC. I spotted one from John Lambertus in California. John was the resident DNA manager for the McIntosh family and suggested that I look at my FTDNA account and check my Y matches. The reason? Gary's results had arrived. By the tone of John's e-mail, the results must have been good.

I opened my FTDNA account to my Y results, and there it was: Gary was at the top of my matches list. The genetic distance was a −2 out of 111 markers. Prior to this, the closest match was −9. I double checked what that meant. Sure enough, he was estimated to be very closely related. And because of the "McIntosh" book, I knew he was my fourth cousin. The common ancestor was our third great-grandfather, Donald Gilbert. I had confirmed McIntosh as my surname!

I called Connie McKenzie to share the news. She started as my mentor in Y testing and became a good friend in the process. Because of her training, I had learned to interpret what the results meant. At the same time, I wanted Connie's confirmation as well. She had encouraged and pushed me not to settle for anything less than solid Y DNA proof about any surname. Only with a close match in Y testing would Connie agree that I had found the right surname. Lately, she had been worried that I was overly convinced that McIntosh was "the one."

I dialed her number and she answered. "Hi, Connie. Gary's test results have posted, and I would like you to look at them and tell me what you think." Since I already knew the answer, it would be interesting to hear her response. There was a moment's silence. Then it sounded like she was crying. Finally, she began to speak. "You're a McIntosh! Do you realize you're a McIntosh???" Connie's excited response was music to my ears. I said, "Yes Connie, I do realize I am a McIntosh." She was truly thrilled for me. There was no doubt that I was now and had always been a McIntosh. This was a momentary victory as I waited for the three tests that would identify Stuart as my father.

JUNE 8, 2015

The Scottish Country Shop in Portland was my next destination and ordering a kilt was my next objective. On the way there, my mind flashed back to the many times I'd visited that business. On my first visit, I mentioned I was adopted and searching for my birth father. I said that he was more than likely Scottish. The employees on duty asked, "When are you going to buy your kilt?" My reply: "When I know my father's clan." With each subsequent visit, the employees asked the same question, and I'd give them the same answer. Before I knew it, that original question took the place of "Hello" each time I stopped in. Many times, I stopped in just to feel a wee bit of Scotland.

Today was different. Today when I opened the shop door I proclaimed, "I am ready to order my kilt!" Gordon and Sean, employees of the shop almost fainted. A second later, with grins on their faces, they took my measurements. After I looked at McIntosh tartan samples, I chose the traditional pattern, which carried a distinctive look in bold shades of red, green, and blue.

Sean said it would take eight to twelve weeks for the kilt to be made and shipped to the shop from Scotland. They would notify me when it arrived. I was fine with that. It gave me ample time to purchase the accessories and learn what it meant to be a McIntosh. By dressing in the kilt of my heritage, I would honor both my father and our family.

JUNE 9, 2015

Gary called and invited Diana and I over to his home the next evening. It was a chance for us to get to get acquainted, learn more about the McIntoshes, and look at family pictures. He was doing his part by reaching out and being inclusive.

JUNE 10, 2015

Diana and I had a great time getting to know Gary and his wife Nancy. As we drove up to his home, he waved to us from his deck in welcome. He offered us something to drink. We sat around the table and looked at a number of family pictures. Finally, he came to the showstopper…there was William McIntosh, the face that launched my McIntosh era. Exuberantly, Gary blurted out, "He looks more like my great-grandfather than I do! He could be William's brother!" Gary and I didn't share many physical similarities, but our energy levels and personalities were almost identical.

THE NEWPORT COMMITMENT

JUNE 15, 2015

Three months ago, the All-Ireland Cultural Society had agreed to be a part of the Newport Celtic Festival held on the Oregon coast in the second week of June. I had been a member of the society for over a year and persuaded them to be a part of this year's event. I was one of five members that staffed the society's booth. A year ago, Diana and I had attended the festival for the first time. I came knowing only that I was ethnically Scottish or Irish. As we walked through the Clan tents, tasted the food, heard the music, smelled the haggis and watched the highland games, the feeling of being home came over me. But as to which culture, I wasn't sure. I left that event in a quandary. I enjoyed it, but what was I?

This time, I was Scottish and very close to identifying my father. Every piece of evidence pointed in Stuart's direction. I had arrived in Newport on Friday to help set up the exhibit that evening. Jim O'Connell, president of the club, was staying at the same motel. We had become good friends, and I enjoyed his company. After setup was completed, we headed to the Irish pub in town for a bite to eat.

The next morning, the weather was cloudy and breezy. I had borrowed a utility kilt, Ghillie shirt, and socks to wear while manning the booth at the festival. Jim had done the same. Since I had never worn any of this before, I went over to Jim's room to ask him how to put on the kilt. After he had given me instructions, I went back to my room and closed the curtains.

I wanted to make sure that my first attempt at wearing a kilt was a private affair. I struggled a bit, and finally I was ready as I would ever be. As I opened the door to head for Jim's room, I did what every kilt wearing newbie would do. I checked to see if anyone was around. The coast was clear and I made a beeline for Jim's door. I knocked. Jim opened the door dressed in his kilt. He approved of the way I looked, and we headed for the festival location.

By the time we reached the festival parking area, I felt a little more at ease. We parked the car and walked onto the festival grounds. I started counting the number of men wearing kilts and they definitely outnumbered those not wearing one. I knew I was safe to proudly wear mine. It was 8:30 a.m. and the gates opened at nine o'clock. I used the next twenty minutes to briskly walk through the different areas of activity.

A number of clans had exhibit space as well. Clan MacKintosh of North America was one of them. I walked over and met the representative. Our conversation turned to my new clan. With pride, he dramatized a colorful history of the MacKintoshes. After he finished, I shared a brief version of my story. I asked about membership in Clan MacKintosh of North America. I could tell he was excited. He handed me an application for membership to fill out. I thanked him and returned later with the finished form. I had taken another step in connecting with my heritage—it felt terrific!

At noon, I took Diana to lunch. She had driven down with our friend, Sally, to join me for the day. By the time Diana arrived, I had grown comfortable in wearing my kilt and looking like a Scotsman. At first, Diana didn't know what to say when she saw the "new" me.

We decided on a seafood restaurant near the ocean in Newport. As we entered the eating establishment, I spied seven (I counted them) other men being manly themselves, dressed in their kilts. I said to Diana while pointing, "See, there are other men dressed in kilts here." She agreed and slowly warmed up to the idea of me wearing one.

While Bruce, Sheila, Jim, and Louise of the Irish club engaged festival goers in conversations related to Ireland's heritage, customs, and family history, I spent most of my time talking with attendees about DNA testing. My message was to use testing to supercharge genealogy, to solve mysteries in family trees, and to aid adoptees in searching for their birth families. This was highlighted by the drawing to win a free DNA test, sponsored by the club.

During the course of the festival, I had spoken to over three hundred people about DNA testing. In my mind, it had been a successful, but tiring experience. About an hour before closing on the second day, a woman and her husband stopped and asked what was involved in DNA testing. I explained how it's used in genetic genealogy and focused on benefits to adoptees when searching for birth parents. Their interest seemed to increase with each new sentence.

When I finished, the woman asked, "Do you have an example of an adoptee that successfully found their birth parents using this method?" Did I have an example?

"Yes, I do. I found my birth father through DNA testing." Her eyes lit up. I couldn't resist. "Would you like me to share my story with you?" "Absolutely!" they exclaimed.

She and her husband listened intently and studied each picture as I happily shared the details of my journey. I told them that I was waiting on three tests for confirmation, but was quite sure I had the right person. About twenty other festival-goers had gathered to listen as well.

Then the unexpected happened. Immediately after I finished speaking, she reached over, hugged me, and began to sob. I didn't understand why this was happening or what to do about it. Had I said something that caused her to cry? And the weirdest part? As I looked at her husband, he softly said, "Thank you" more than once. What was going on?

She gently pulled away as she regained her composure. What she said next left me speechless. "I had the feeling I needed to be at the Celtic Festival today, but wasn't sure why. I now know it was to talk with you." My attention was now focused on her. She was looking directly at me as she continued. "I was adopted and didn't have the best experience. The idea of searching for my birth family never seemed possible. But as I listened to your story, I realized there was hope." She made me promise to write a book and tell my story to everyone that would listen. I was in Newport sharing my story. I had toyed with the idea of writing a book, but up until now I had not seriously considered it.

After thanking me, she left to look at the other exhibits. The other Irish club members were as blown away as I was about what had happened. The same couple returned three more times to hug and thank me. Her words had left their mark on my heart. By the end of the day, I made a commitment to write my book, and share my story whenever the opportunity presented itself. Now, I knew my real purpose for being there as well.

Meeting and waiting

June 18, 2015

I made my annual trip to California. On my itinerary were visits to Nancy's brother, Tom, his wife, Mary Bell, my brother, Malcolm, and John Lambertus. He would be my second encounter with a McIntosh. In past conversations, John was always friendly and eagerly shared information and documentation about the McIntosh family. Now we had the chance to meet in person, and I was looking forward to it.

Since reuniting with Nancy in 2001, I had made at least one trip a year to visit Nancy, Malcolm, Tom, and his wife, Mary Bell. But this visit had a different feel to it. What was the difference? I was a McIntosh on the verge of confirming Stuart as my birth father.

My brother, aunt, and uncle were captivated by the new information I shared. They had been so supportive through it all. Mary Bell could hardly wait to find out if Stuart was my father and told me so. Tom and Malcolm weren't as demonstrative but just as interested. And each night before bed, I faithfully checked my FTDNA account for the results of my two second cousins. Nothing showed up. Two days before my return to Portland, I drove down to meet John in person and have lunch at his home.

He met me at a shopping center that we agreed upon. John and I hugged, got in his car, and drove back to his residence. What struck me about John was his red hair and fair complexion. He was soft spoken and accommodating. It was a sunny day, and his home and accompanying view reminded me of a scene from *Sunset* magazine. As we sat eating lunch on his patio, the conversation focused on our immediate families. His wife had joined us for the meal, and we immediately found common ground—our love of chocolate!

John was the perfect host—cook, waiter, and receptionist. After finishing lunch, we headed into the living room and looked at family photos on the TV. He had his PC hooked up to the flat screen. Every detail in each picture was clear. Some of the family I had seen before, but there were many that were new to me. John was able to identify every person and share a story about each. When it was time to leave, John cheerfully drove me back to my car. On the way back to Tom's, one thought lingered. I had experienced family with John.

JUNE 21, 2015
After saying good-bye to Tom, Mary Bell, and Malcolm, I drove back to the Sacramento airport, checked in, and waited for my flight to return home. For the last thirteen years, my maternal family had consistently shown love and inclusion, and this trip was no different. John continued what Gary began—a warm welcome to my new paternal family. If this was a preview of things to come, I was looking forward to future interactions with the McIntosh clan.

I flew home on Father's Day. During the ninety-minute flight, I thought about the past. As a child, our family celebrated the occasion, and it seemed a happy time. As I got older, the bondless relationship with my adopted father became increasingly painful. Father's Day became a day I wanted to forget. A false, hollow quality was associated with even the thought of it.

Very shortly that could all change. My only wish this Father's Day was to have seen my second cousins' test results appear, confirming Stuart my father before I left California. I had checked each day—nothing showed up yet. How much longer would it be before they arrived? Would I get my wish?

JUNE 22, 2015

I was home. After I unpacked and ate breakfast, I headed to my PC and checked each of my DNA accounts with Ancestry, FTDNA, and 23andMe. After I viewed Ancestry and 23andMe, FTDNA was next. About two-thirds of the way down on my first page of matches, there it was - one of my second cousins' test results had been posted. He was my second cousin! And right below that was the other one. Both had matched me as second cousins, which made Stuart my father. Or should I say "my Dad"?

Stuart was my father. And my cousins' results…I couldn't help but stare at them. I was overjoyed and yet, the last test remained unaccounted for: Keith's. Was he my first cousin? Even though the second cousins' results proved Stuart was my father, Keith's would be the icing on the DNA cake. Emotionally, I still had doubts. He was my closest link to Stuart. I needed to know.

STUART, THE MAN

APRIL 24, 2015

What did I know about Stuart? In March, I received a copy of his obituary, courtesy of Robert Ligouri. It was time to review the information. The document read: *"J.H. Stuart "Stu" McIntosh, age 79 of Roseburg, Oregon, passed away Friday, December 26, 2008. He was born in Lamont, Canada to Keith Louden and Margaret Ila (Murray) McIntosh. The family moved from Kamsack, Saskatchewan, Canada to Corvallis, Oregon in 1937."*

Stuart had attended elementary, junior, and senior high school, and his first year of college in Corvallis. He served in the military from August 1948, returning home on August 1, 1950. Nancy got pregnant in the middle of that month. Stuart got a job with the forest service during the first part of September and left shortly thereafter to man the lookouts used as fire watches in the Cascade Mountains. He never returned to Corvallis other than to visit his parents on occasion.

After working for the forest service, Stuart was employed at The Dalles Dam on the Columbia River and later worked for Pacific Power and Light in the Portland area. For the next thirty-two years, he remained with the company. During that time, Stuart was transferred to Cottage Grove in 1973, then to his final location of Roseburg in 1977, and retired in 1989. Stuart remained in Roseburg until his passing in 2008.

Two things became very apparent. Stuart more than likely wasn't aware of Nancy's pregnancy and never had any biological offspring. Keith had told me that Stuart considered him to be "the son that he and Delores could never have." (Delores was his first wife.) His second wife, Bette, brought two children into the relationship from her previous marriage. I wondered about the effect that had on Stuart. Compounding this was him never knowing about my existence. The impact of having been his only biological child overwhelmed me. Would my life have turned out different if he had known?

Markers and memories

After reviewing Stuart's obituary, I decided to get in contact with his stepchildren, Joanne and Steve, if it was possible. As of 2008, they were both living in the Eugene area. Since their mother, Bette, had died in 2010 and meeting Stuart wasn't an option, her children were the most likely to have knowledge as to what type of man Stuart was. What kind of reception would I receive?

The next morning, I searched for the phone numbers of Joanne and Steve. The idea of getting their perspective on Stuart interested me greatly. When he married Bette in 1973, Joanne was twenty-five and Steve twenty, respectively. By my math, they had known him for thirty-five years. It was safe to say they knew more about him than any other person living. As of 2015, both were still listed in the Eugene phone directory.

I located Joanne's number first and made the call. Would anyone be home or answer the phone? How would my call be received? I waited for an answer. A man's voice greeted me, and I asked for Joanne by name. "Just a minute. I'll get her." A moment later, she answered with a very warm tone to her voice.

After our initial greetings, I asked if her mother had been married to Stuart McIntosh, to which she replied affirmatively. I continued by explaining the reason for my call. I then asked, "Would you mind if I told you my story? It's a bit unusual." Joanne said, "Sure, go ahead." After I explained how Stuart came to be my father, she responded in such a way that caught me off guard. "That's terrific, and I'm so happy for you. Stuart was a wonderful man, and I loved him."

Wait a minute, why was she so happy for me and why was he so wonderful? Most of the stepchildren I knew had less than favorable opinions of their stepparents. She then answered the question in my mind by saying, "I should tell you that my brother and I are adopted as well. I reconnected with my birth family years ago." She got it—Joanne knew exactly what I was going through and what it meant to find my father.

Joanne continued. "Stuart treated me like his own daughter and I know he would have loved having a son." Oh my gosh! It took a moment for her last words to sink in: "He would have *loved* having a son." That phrase led me to believe that if Stuart had known of Nancy's pregnancy, he very likely would have taken responsibility and my life could have turned out quite differently. This revelation would have powerfully impacted both of us as father and son.

Before the call ended, Joanne and I had agreed to meet on Saturday. I informed Diana about the conversation and prepared an itinerary for the trip south. Our first stop would be to visit Stuart's grave, located at the National Military cemetery in Roseburg, Oregon, about 180 miles away. Another stop would be at Stuart's home. Joanne had given me the address for both. On our return trip home, we would stop in Eugene at a local restaurant to meet Joanne and her husband, Roger. I had asked her if she would be willing to write down her memories of Stuart to go along with the pictures she had offered to share. She enthusiastically agreed to do so.

JUNE 28, 2015

I was ready for tomorrow. Visiting Stuart's final resting place would give me the opportunity to see and touch something that physically represented this man. And what would Joanne tell me? There would be much to process emotionally. I wanted to experience this event moment by moment.

JUNE 29, 2015

As we traveled toward Roseburg, Diana and I reviewed our plans for the day.

I wasn't sure emotionally how this would play out. In a way, it seemed similar to when I first met Nancy. The obvious difference was Nancy had been alive. I felt on some level that I would vicariously meet Stuart for the first time.

Once in Roseburg, we followed the directions I got on the Internet from Mapquest. We had some trouble finding the street that led to the cemetery. Diana called the cemetery office to clear up our confusion. A woman answered. I spoke with her using my phone's connection in our car. "We are here to visit Stuart McIntosh's grave. Can you tell us how to get there?" She said, "Let me check to see which cemetery he is buried in." So, there was more than one military cemetery. That was a good thing to know. She said, "He is located in the older one." She gave us directions, including the exact location of his marker.

As we neared our destination, I saw the sign to turn into the cemetery. My heart was beating a bit faster as I made the left turn into the entrance. The parking lot was immediately to our left. We found a place to park. Before getting out of the car, Diana asked if I wanted to be alone with Stuart once I had found the marker. I hadn't even thought of that. I said, "Yes, that would be great." It turned out to be a wise decision. We opened the car doors to a beautiful day. There wasn't a cloud in the sky, and the temperature was ideal. The grounds were beautifully kept, and in spite of a major thoroughfare running next to the cemetery, it was relatively quiet. As far as I could tell, we had the cemetery to ourselves.

I had been told that Stuart's marker was near the flagpole, next to the parking lot we had just parked in. I had spotted the flagpole as we neared the cemetery and was now looking directly at it. Within three minutes, I had found the marker. Diana had brought her camera along and said she was going to walk around and take pictures. "How much time do you think you'll need?" "I don't know, give me about fifteen minutes." That was just a guess. No matter how long I stayed that day, it wouldn't be enough.

As I stared down at Stuart's marker, my emotions began to surface. The feeling of loss prevailed in my mind and heart as the tears began to fall. I thought of all that we could have shared—our love of music, learning about his love for sports, hiking together in the Cascade mountains, sharing precious father–son time, and the love we would have shared with each other. I then noticed something that affected me deeply. Below his name on the marker, the military rank of corporal at the time of being honorably discharged from the US Army was inscribed. I too had served in the army and held that same rank upon being discharged twenty-four years later. By then, the tears were flowing freely. Tears of sadness, yes, but also tears of joy. I felt a tangible bond beginning to build between the two of us.

One of my final thoughts before leaving stood out as one of the most poignant. Stuart would never get to know his grandchildren. I wanted to pull up a bench and stay longer. The day was perfect, and a father–son talk was long overdue. As I turned toward the parking lot to leave, Diana had returned from her picture taking adventure and asked if I would stand next to the flagpole. She wanted to document our visit to Stuart's final resting place. I wasn't usually a willing participant but decided this experience needed to be captured in pictures. "Are you ready to go?" Wanting to stay, but needing to go, I responded, "Yes." There would be other visits.

Meeting Joanne

Our next stop was the home Stuart had shared with his wife, Bette. I had been given the address by Joanne. We had an easier time locating the house than the cemetery. We found ourselves in a neatly kept group of homes in a subdivision. The idea of talking to neighbors that might have known Stuart crossed my mind. Diana must have been thinking the same thing and asked, "I wonder if any of the neighbors are home?" "It sure doesn't look like it," was my reply. We stayed in the car while she took pictures of Stuart's home from the passenger's side. With that portion of our journey now completed, we headed for Eugene to rendezvous with Joanne and Roger.

We had agreed to meet at a restaurant located on the Willamette River. She and I had traded descriptions of each other to make identification easier. Joanne said she would be easy to spot, due to her height. I responded by telling her to look for my bright blue "McIntosh" T-shirt I'd be proudly wearing. Joanne's comment: "Well. That ought to be easy to spot."

By mid-afternoon, we arrived at the restaurant. There were very few cars in the parking lot. Inside, I counted as many customers as cars. Before we were seated, using Joanne's description as a visual reference, I asked the hostess if another couple had arrived. We were seated at a booth that was visible from the entrance. Everything was in place. But even though Joanne and Roger's entry would be easy to spot, the temptation to stare in that direction was hard to resist. While we waited, I mentally reviewed all the questions I wanted to ask.

About fifteen minutes later, a couple entered, with the woman matching Joanne's description. I was sure they saw my shirt. We waved at them, and they reciprocated. As they approached, I overheard Roger say, "Boy, he sure reminds me of Stuart." I was taken by surprise. What would cause him to say that? It hadn't occurred to me that resemblances were more than just physical similarities. Gestures, mannerisms, speech patterns, and inflections played a role as well. Roger's seven words set the tone of our first meeting.

Our introductions happened while Joanne and Roger were being seated. It was good to finally meet. They seemed to be genuinely nice people. "Here, I have something for you." She reached over and handed me a manila packet. I quickly opened it and glanced inside. Pages of pictures and the written memories of Stuart I had requested caught my eye. Diana was excited to look over the contents. I, on the other hand, launched into a conversation with Joanne almost immediately.

I began with a recap of my story, interspersed with family pictures and genetic genealogical research I'd accumulated over the length of my journey. Both Joanne and Roger seemed interested and listened intently. Diana, on the other hand, was more than familiar with my tale. Knowing our conversation would go on for a while, she gently broke in and asked to look through the contents of the manila packet. Since she had my story memorized, looking through the packet would keep her occupied. I handed it to her. There would be time to view the pictures and memorabilia later.

In the meantime, I hurried to finish my story. I was anxious to hear about Joanne's relationship with Stuart. She started by sharing the love she had for him. To me, this was a testament regarding the character of Stuart, the man I would never meet. She then echoed what Roger had said when approaching our table upon arrival—how much I reminded her of Stuart. There were tears in her eyes. Joanne wasn't saying this to make me feel good, her tears and feelings were genuine!

Then Joanne spoke about Stuart's love of music, jazz in particular. Nancy had loved jazz as well. Although I couldn't prove it, I believe jazz is what brought them together. Corvallis most likely had a place where jazz was played, either live or over the radio, and the two of them ended up together because of it. Before she finished, Joanne had painted a picture of a good man who loved jazz, baseball, music, family, and serving the community in various capacities. The vicarious bonding between Stuart and me continued to grow.

Our time together was up before we knew it. As we got up to leave, Diana pulled out her camera and asked Joanne, Roger, and me to pose for pictures in the lobby. That was followed by hugs and good-byes. While hugging Joanne, I thanked her for meeting with us. "I love you for making this possible." And as Aunt Margaret had said to me, I then told Joanne, with a slight change from the original, "This makes you my stepsister." She agreed. Hugs to remember that moment, and pictures for remembering later.

On our way home, I thought about all that the day had meant. For Joanne, I was an extension of Stuart, a man she truly loved and admired. For me, I had bonded with someone that had known and loved my father for thirty-five years. Joanne and her brother, Steve, were the two that knew Stuart better than anyone else alive. It then occurred to me that maybe this was as healing for her as it was for me. An unforgettable experience had just happened.

Just before I went to bed, one final thought awakened that had never occurred before. During this journey to find my father Stuart, I am learning what it means to honor my family surname. I had felt honor upon knowing that Stuart was my father. Upon seeing his marker in the cemetery, the word "honor" took on new meaning. We both had served our country with honor. I knew the importance of representing the name of McIntosh with honor. And now, I wanted to honor my father by becoming the type of individual he had been.

THREE HOURS TO FIND MY GRANDPARENTS

JULY 14, 2015

Something was missing. I hadn't the foggiest idea as to where Keith and Margaret McIntosh were buried. In fact, I had very little in the way of information or pictures regarding either one. I had their names, birth and death dates, location and marriage record. Through reading my "McIntosh" book, I had learned that Stuart's parents had sold their creamery business in Corvallis in 1955 and moved to Salem, Oregon, in 1956. Where were they buried, and where were their obituaries? Keith had died in April 1973 and Margaret in December 1978. Since they had died in Salem, the most likely source for answers was the *Statesman Journal*, the local newspaper.

Then an impulsive idea struck me. That afternoon, I had three hours open in my schedule. Why not go on a road trip to Salem? Maybe I'd get lucky and find copies of their obituaries in the local paper. I decided to travel to the main library in downtown Salem. Did I have enough time to actually pull this off?

Most public libraries carried archived copies of the local newspaper on microfilm, and in this case, the Salem *Statesman Journal* would have printed the obituaries. I had never been to the Salem Public Library, but I did have directions courtesy of Mapquest. It took me close to an hour to get to the library and find a place to park. I kept thinking I'd probably run out of time before I accomplished my mission. There were two hours left.

I entered the library and found the information desk. I asked about archived *Statesman Journal* issues and was told they were over with the microfilm machines. To save time, I asked the woman at the information counter to help load the film. She offered her services. Eagerly, I agreed to let her proceed. Knowing the dates of their deaths, I easily found the film that corresponded. Once she had set the film into position, I began to search by date. In about ten minutes, I had found the obituaries for my grandparents, Keith and Margaret McIntosh. A copy machine was conveniently connected to the microfilm equipment. After I had made a couple of copies of each obituary, I looked at the library clock...I completed the task in twenty minutes. One hour and forty minutes were left. Back in the car, I read through their obituaries and spotted an unexpected piece of information—the name of the church they had attended while living in Salem. How would I locate the church?

I was sure that Salem had a visitor's center, so I drove to the center of downtown and looked for signs. I spotted one almost immediately. I turned left at the corner, and there it was. Parking my car about a block away, I entered the building. "Can I help you?" the woman behind the counter said cheerfully. "Yes, my grandparents were members of the First United Methodist Church. Do you happen to know where it is located?" She looked directly at me and pointed. "If you turn around and look out the window, the church is the big brick one about a block away." What I saw was unbelievable. Not only was I looking at the church, but I had parked my car right in front of it! If I had looked more closely at the surroundings when I got out of the car, the sign for the church would've been clearly visible.

Before I left the visitor's center, I asked if she knew where the mortuaries listed in the obituaries were located. "Sure, one is about a mile away from here." She gave me directions and I thanked her. Hurrying out of the door, I made my way to the church office. Before entering, I realized that I'd recognized this church from seeing it as a child when taking trips to Salem. The steeple was one of the tallest and most distinctive landmarks in the downtown area. This structure took on a whole new meaning for me. My grandparents must have walked this ground I was standing on many years earlier.

I found the office open and told the church secretary that my grandparents had been members there. I asked if they had any records, documents, and pictures that might have been kept in the church archives. She made copies of the obituaries I was carrying. "If we find anything, we'll mail it to you." I gave her my address, thanked her, and proceeded back to my car. Twenty more minutes had passed. Dang it! I really wished that more time was available. I was in the same building that my grandparents had been in fifty years earlier and time wasn't permitting me to linger.

I drove to the mortuary parking lot where my grandfather Keith's services were held, which was one mile away. "Can I help you?" A man greeted me at the front desk. "I was wondering if you could tell me where my grandfather Keith McIntosh is buried." I explained that his service had been performed there in 1973. "Just a minute, I'll check our records." He confirmed that they had done the services and called the company that handled the cremation. There was a new piece of the puzzle. I then assumed that both Keith and Margaret had been cremated. After the receptionist hung up the phone, he gave me the answer. "Your grandfather is interned in the cemetery on the hill. Turn right out of the parking lot, go one mile, and turn right. At the top of the hill, it's on the right."

Never being much of a risk taker, I decided to become one. I had the feeling that both of my grandparents were interred at the same cemetery. Margaret had a different mortuary listed in her obituary, but quite likely was in the same location. Ten more minutes had passed.

One mile and a hill later, I pulled into the main gate of the cemetery and spotted the office on the right. I parked and went inside. Would I find someone to help me? No one was in the receptionist's area. I heard voices in an adjacent room to my left. I didn't want to interrupt what was going on. Time was running out. After waiting a few minutes, I decided to begin searching on my own. Just as I was ready to leave the office an employee came through the main door. "Can I help you?" "Yes, my grandfather is interred here, and I don't know where he's located." The man was to the point. "What's his name?" I said two words. "Keith McIntosh." "McIntosh, huh? Well, I'm Scottish too. In fact, there are a lot of Scots here!" His Scottish pride really showed as he spoke those words. In a few seconds, he'd found what he was looking for and said, "Follow me, He's in the mausoleum. I'll take you right to the spot." Once again, I had been amazed how quickly things were happening.

The mausoleum was just across the street from the office. Within one minute, we were standing in the center of the building. "Here he is, and it looks like his wife is next to him. Have a good day." I thanked him as he left. I was all alone with my grandparents. To commemorate this experience, I took a couple of pictures with my phone, and then decided to sit for a moment. I marveled at what had transpired. In less than two hours, I had been successful in finding the obituaries, locating the church, visiting the mortuary, and viewing my grandparents' resting place. Gratitude filled my thoughts as I headed home, with time to spare.

JULY 22, 2015

A package came this morning. It was from the First United Methodist Church in Salem. Taking it into the kitchen, I excitedly grabbed a knife and opened one end. The contents had to contain information about my grandparents. I slid the paperwork onto the table. There were articles about Keith and Margaret's involvement in church activities, documentation about their membership, and a newspaper clipping with a picture of my grandmother. An accompanying article told about the luncheon she had hosted in her home for a women's group in 1970. Wow! So that was what Margaret looked like. It was a side view, but I saw some resemblance, especially around her eyes. A talent she possessed was featured behind her on the wall. In the article, it mentioned that the painting was one of her originals. She was an artist. I had minored in art during my years in college. DNA had struck again. Margaret had passed her talent down to me. The article also mentioned that she had won a baking contest and was serving her winning recipe to those in attendance. I trained as a chef in the military and worked in a restaurant to earn money while in college. The only thing missing was a picture of Keith.

Later that day, I began thinking again about the tests taken by my second cousins. Technically, I had proven Stuart to be my father. I had been excited, but I still felt incomplete. My probable Canadian cousin Keith's results would give me the emotional peace of mind I'd been looking for. On top of that, I still hadn't heard whether he'd taken the new test, not to mention mailing it in. I had done everything possible to confirm the identity of both my mother and father and yet, without Keith's results, the hole that represented my unknown father would never be totally filled.

The unexpected relatives arrived

July 28, 2015

A new second cousin match appeared on Ancestry today. Who in the heck was he? This match snuck in right under my DNA nose. There was a sizeable family tree included. I looked at the surnames and found that he was definitely linked to Margaret McIntosh's Murray/Stanley lines. Upon inspection, I found that his grandmother, Addie May Murray, was the older sister of Margaret, my grandmother. Here was a paternal bonus I hadn't expected. I promptly messaged him, introduced myself and verified the information in his tree.

August 7, 2015

Jim Crozier, my new Murray second cousin, and I had been exchanging messages. He not only confirmed the information on Ancestry, but was willing to send hard copies from the Murray/Stanley family-history book. Wow, that would be the second family-history book given to me. Again, I had no hesitation in saying "Yes!"

AUGUST 10, 2015

I had Jim's results, so I decided to run some numbers. The range of cMs[**] needed for a second cousin match was from 101 to 375. My McIntosh second cousins came in at 162. Jim's results were at 395. His were way above the average, while the others substantially lower, but still acceptable—one more piece of DNA evidence in favor of Stuart.

A MYSTERY SOLVED

AUGUST 12, 2015

I got the feeling that I needed to review something. Three months earlier, I had discovered three matches on Ancestry that were estimated to be third to fourth cousins. There was a small family tree with one that hadn't yielded any common surnames. A week ago, I took another look and got the feeling that a surname might have been overlooked. I messaged Wilma Hoover again, asking if any surname had been left off her list.

Wilma wrote back and said the only name she might have forgotten was MacArthur. MacArthur? That surname figured prominently in McIntosh family history. I asked if I might phone her. She said, sure anytime. I was pumped. Maybe the answer to my mystery was a phone call away. I called, and Wilma answered. "I believe I remember the name of the MacArthur. It was Mary, and her husband was James Young." "Oh, honey, let me call you back. I need to pull out the 'Young' family book to make sure that's right."

[**]   CentiMorgan was the term given results to measure how much DNA was shared between matches. The more centiMorgans shared, the closer the match relationship-wise.

After she hung up, I pulled out my trusted *"MacKintosh"* Book and looked at the MacArthur pedigree chart. To be perfectly honest, I had never really focused on the MacArthurs, other than the name of my great-great-grandmother and her direct ancestral line that went back to 1700. I located my great-great-grandmother, Christina MacArthur, first wife of Archibald McIntosh, my great-great-grandfather. Christina, born in 1848, was the oldest of seven siblings. It was time to meet them.

Starting with Christina, I went down the line and slowly read each name. I stopped in my tracks. The best had been saved for last. I stared at the name: Mary MacArthur. And right below hers was the name of her husband, James Young. I screamed! Diana had been in the kitchen and came to see if I'd hurt myself. "What's going on?" "I just solved the mystery as to the identity of the three Ancestry matches!" She chalked it up to momentary craziness. I was ecstatic. In my studio, I studied the details on Mary.

Mary was born in Ontario, Canada, in 1860, making her twelve years younger than Christina. The other siblings were born one or two years apart from each other. The McIntosh family was living in the same area during that time frame. The name, date, and location lined up perfectly. I beat Wilma to the punch and called her back first. She answered, "Hello?" "Wilma, you did it. You make a great Sherlock Holmes. Mary MacArthur is my second great grandmother's younger sister!" Then Wilma said something very interesting. "I was hoping you were related to me. This is my husband's side of the family!"

She was truly happy for me and glad she could help. With Wilma's assistance, I had figured it out. Wilma's son and daughter were my third cousins once removed, and her granddaughter, third cousin twice removed. This was a great example of how genetic genealogy solved a family mystery when traditional means fell short.

Celtic Games and meeting Steve

About two weeks ago, I realized that I hadn't contacted Stuart's stepson Steve. For some reason, that had slipped my mind. Finding his phone number, I made the call. Joanne's recollections had been positive. I was really interested as to what Steve would say. The answering machine greeted me, and I left a message, including my phone number. Would he return my call?

A day later, he left a message on my phone, including the best times to call. It was my turn. The third time was the charm. A woman answered. I asked for Steve, and she said, "Just a moment." Steve picked up the receiver, and our conversation began. I gave Steve a rundown of my connection to Stuart. He seemed really interested and supportive. His reaction was very similar to Joanne's. We talked about getting together. Checking my calendar, I noticed that the Douglas County Celtic Highland Games were happening on August 15. I asked Steve if that date worked for him. He said that date would be fine. We agreed to meet at 5:00 p.m. That gave us time to go to the Celtic Highland Games in Roseburg, Oregon. Since Stuart had lived in Roseburg, I planned on asking some of the festival organizers if they had known or heard of him.

Today, Diana and I made our second three-hour road trip south to Roseburg that summer. I spent a lot of my travel time wondering what Steve would say. Once again, the weather was perfect. The games were held each August in the neighboring town of Winston. As we drove up, it looked like quite a few people were at the games. Because of that, we ended up parking a fair distance away. The exercise was welcomed after sitting three hours in the car.

The location for the games was ideal, and the good weather empha-sized it. Diana and I decided to peruse the entire layout. The clans were well represented, the sword fight was authentically recreated both in attire and equipment, and of course, an array of Scottish delicacies tempted the attendees. Again, I felt very much at home here. After a beautiful afternoon of Celtic fun, it was time to head for Eugene. I had asked a number of people about Stuart, and no one seemed to know anything about him. Since Stuart had been active in community affairs, I was hoping to speak to someone who knew him. I was really disappointed to have come up empty-handed. I wanted to stay longer, but meeting with Steve was more important.

We arrived at Steve's in just over an hour. We would have been there sooner had it not been for a couple of navigational errors. Not knowing what kind of reception might be in store for us, we were pleasantly surprised by the one given. Steve came out to greet us at our car. After a warm welcome, he invited us in and we met his wife, Sue. They motioned for us to sit at the dining room table where they had some refreshments waiting for us.

After we were seated, Steve and Sue wanted a longer version of my story. But before I started, Sue said, "We will tell you the unvarnished truth about Stuart." I responded, "That sounds good." I felt uneasy and wanted to keep a positive spin on things. What was I in for? As soon as I had finished my story, they began sharing their memories of Stuart. Sue started. "Stuart was a wonderful man." My initial uneasiness turned to anticipation for their next words. As Steve and Sue shared their memories, I pictured a genuinely nice guy. At one point, Sue mentioned how much I reminded her of Stuart. Steve echoed her comment. "You really do remind me of Stuart." There were tears in his eyes as he spoke. I was truly touched by this. Sue had gathered together a number of mementos for us to take home. "These are for you." "Are you sure about that?" I asked. "Absolutely," she said convincingly. Included was a scrapbook relating to Stuart's employment, a Bible that was given to him by his mother, Margaret, and twenty slides, which included Stuart as a baby, teenager, during his stint in the army, and during the time he was married to Bette, his second wife. I wanted the slides made into prints.

Their generosity had overwhelmed me. I noticed it was starting to get dark, and we still had two hours of driving left. The time had flown by. We agreed to keep in touch. As I hugged Steve, I said softly, "I have a new step-brother." He nodded in approval. Diana took pictures of Steve, Sue, and me to visually document our visit. I felt more than satisfied about the events of the day.

On our return trip to Portland, I reviewed everything said about Stuart by Steve and Sue. Their recollections were stunningly close to Joanne's, especially considering that Steve and Joanne hadn't spoken to each other before our visit. Stuart had become my role model. By his example, he was showing how to be a better husband, father, grandfather, and friend through the words, images, and feelings shared by those who knew him best.

FIVE DISTRACTIONS BEFORE THE TEST RESULTS

AUGUST 28, 2015

Keith e-mailed to let me know he'd taken the test, and it was headed for Houston. Hallelujah! Six to eight weeks stood between me and the posting of Keith's results. The long wait of over six months would finally be over. I remembered the good that came out of the extraordinary amount of time I had waited for that moment. I learned to look for others to test in case Keith's test never materialized. I was introduced to my second cousins who tested and proved Stuart to be my father. Without that delay, I would have never pushed to look for others who could test in place of Keith. The second cousins' confirmations caused Keith's test results to go from "crucial" to "added evidence." In my mind and heart and through my eyes, I viewed Keith's test results as the clincher. The second cousins had proven that Stuart was my father. Even so, complete closure would only come with this last test.

SEPTEMBER 2, 2015

Distractions were always welcome while I waited for test results, but even more so as I waited for Keith's.

The first distraction. USPS had delivered a package from Jim Crozier, my Murray second cousin. Weeks earlier, he had offered to send articles, pictures, and documents pertaining to the Murray and Stanley families. He was more than good for his word. In my hands were family pictures with names and dates, documents of land grants, articles on my Murray ancestors, portraits of my grandmother's sister and my grandmother as a small girl! I e-mailed him my thanks. Words weren't enough for the treasure that he'd sent.

SEPTEMBER 4, 2015

FTDNA notified me that Keith's test had been received. It was in Houston. A sigh of relief left my body knowing part one was complete. The rest was in the testing company's hands. Six to eight weeks to the "R" (results) Day. If we're confirmed as first cousins, Keith would be my closest living McIntosh relative.

SEPTEMBER 7, 2015

The second distraction. Diana and I travelled to Salem and visited the final resting place for Keith and Margaret McIntosh. It was my second time. I had been there earlier, as part of the "Find my grandparents" information in Salem' three-hour adventure. Once again, the weather cooperated. The sun was shining, the temperature was in the midseventies, and the bonus was Diana coming along. With the camera, I was guaranteed better pictures than the ones taken during my first trip down. After we accomplished our mission, time permitted us to make a repeat stop at the church my grandparents had attended. While Diana engaged in another round of picture taking, I took advantage of that and studied the outside of the edifice while I imagined my grandparents walking in the front doors. Once again, the trip home was filled with memories.

The third distraction. Six weeks ago, Diana and I had purchased a DNA test for our son, Doug, from Ancestry. While we waited for his results I said, "Hey, son, soon we'll know what your ethnic makeup is," to which he replied, "Well, first we need to know if *"we"* are related!" Very funny. His sense of humor definitely came from his mother's side of the family. Today, his results arrived. No surprise—he was our son. He also matched all the Blackstones and McIntoshes at the appropriate levels. That was the beauty of DNA testing. The company never knew the identity of the individual testing, or who they might match in their database. With each of my matches who were a second cousin or closer, the results had been consistent with the predicted relationship level.

SEPTEMBER 22, 2015

The fourth distraction. A new first to second cousin match had appeared on Ancestry. I spotted it while talking to Susan Baird. I had learned to multitask. After we finished talking, I investigated more closely as to whom this might be. I had the answer in record time. This match was the uncle of Jim Crozier, making him my first cousin once removed. He was my closest Murray match.

SEPTEMBER 23, 2015

The fifth and final distraction. The Scottish Country Shop called to inform me that my kilt had arrived from Scotland! I went down to the store to pick it up. Sean and Gordon, employees of the store, helped with the initial fitting and explained the importance of wearing it correctly. I noticed that both of them took how one wore a kilt very seriously. As they spoke, I thought of Stuart and how he would feel about his son donning the tartan of our heritage. From that moment on, I regarded my kilt with reverence in honor of the family I had claimed with confidence. Tonight, I wore it to a most appropriate event—a choir rehearsal with the Conchords Chorale. Since music was in the McIntosh DNA, Stuart would've been pleased.

OCTOBER 2, 2015

The wait was finally over. Keith's results had posted. We were first cousins, and I was looking at the results that proved it. Now, I felt complete! The paternal hole I had lived with my entire life was filled. By the numbers, Keith and I shared 854.60 cMs—squarely in the first cousin range. This was as close as I would ever get in confirming Stuart as my father. The roots that connected me to him had been finalized.

THE BIG PICTURE

I took time to mentally rewind and review what had happened. How much time had passed between signing up for the birth registry and confirming Stuart as my father? Twenty years. During that time, I transformed from a child of adoption to an adult in full knowledge of his heritage. Sometimes quickly, and many times at a snail's pace, my journey and quest continued moving forward. When people ask me if this experience was worth it, I always include the following:

My mother wanted to keep me, and my father, had he known, would have moved heaven and earth to find me. The proof? I heard as much from Nancy while she lived, and from Stuart through those who knew him. Was I wanted? Was I loved? Absolutely.

Pedigree Chart

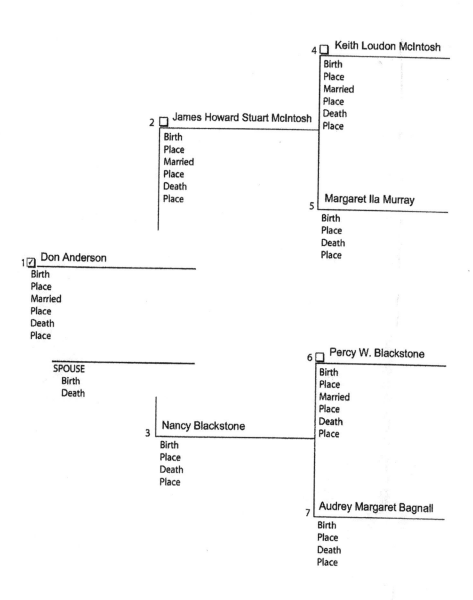

4 ☐ Keith Loudon McIntosh
Birth
Place
Married
Place
Death
Place

2 ☐ James Howard Stuart McIntosh
Birth
Place
Married
Place
Death
Place

5 Margaret Ila Murray
Birth
Place
Death
Place

1 ☑ Don Anderson
Birth
Place
Married
Place
Death
Place

SPOUSE
Birth
Death

6 ☐ Percy W. Blackstone
Birth
Place
Married
Place
Death
Place

3 Nancy Blackstone
Birth
Place
Death
Place

7 Audrey Margaret Bagnall
Birth
Place
Death
Place

8 ☐ Peter Howard McIntosh
Birth
Place
Death
Place

16 ☐ Archibald Wilberforce McIntosh
Birth

17 Christina MacArthur
Birth

9 Margaret L. Shearer
Birth
Place
Death
Place

18 ☐ James M. Shearer
Birth

19 Elizabeth Keith Loudon
Birth

10 ☐ James Murray
Birth
Place
Death
Place

20 ☐ William Murray
Birth

21 Elizabeth 'Betsy' Ross
Birth

11 Adeline Stanley
Birth
Place
Death
Place

22 ☐ James H. Stanley
Birth

23 Mary Jame Douglass
Birth

12 ☐ Perry C. Blackstone
Birth
Place
Death
Place

24 ☐ William S. Blackstone
Birth

25 Sarah Isabelle Porter
Birth

13 Jenny Corrine Wise
Birth
Place
Death
Place

26 ☐ Jacob Wise
Birth

27 Julliette Hudson
Birth

14 ☐ Charles Barker Bagnall
Birth
Place
Death
Place

28 ☐ Charles Bagnall
Birth

29 Anna Ibbs
Birth

15 Stella Mae Peyton
Birth
Place
Death
Place

30 ☐ David Hamilton Peyton
Birth

31 Samantha Ann Willet
Birth

Made in the USA
Columbia, SC
02 August 2018